This accessible yet rich book is a welcome resource for Christian leaders who know well the pressures of their role. Gospel-centred, solidly scriptural, and wrought from ⸻ ⸻ *ig Fresh* reminds the reader of the ⸻ on the only foundation that is secu⸻

Richard Cunningham, Director o⸻

Staying Fresh is exactly the to⸻ ⸻⸺y, overwrought pastors need. The pastoral life is a marathon, not a sprint. Paul Mallard understands that the key to a long and fruitful ministry is less to do with the 'how' and more to do with the 'who'. Character matters more than technical excellence. *Staying Fresh* is an absorbing and personal book, and yet digs deep into the Scriptures to feed the exhausted pastor's soul.
Michael Jensen, Rector of St Mark's Anglican Church, Sydney, Australia, and the author of Is Forgiveness Really Free?

A gem! Another blockbuster from the pen of Paul Mallard.

We all know that the gospel is the most glorious message in the world, but gospel ministry doesn't always feel like that. With a disarming blend of personal experience, good humour, biblical wisdom and pastoral sensitivity, Paul guides pastors and other church leaders through a bewildering maze of issues that threaten to discourage and derail all of us in any kind of church leadership or gospel ministry.

Above all, Paul is a gospel optimist. He keeps bringing us back to the ultimate reality that we're not superman; Jesus is. And he loves church leaders dearly.

Church leaders, this is not a volume to adorn your bookshelves and impress your friends; it is another must-read volume that will enlarge your hearts and enrich your ministries – and, as a result, bless the people you serve.
Richard Underwood, Pastoral Director of FIEC

If you are a leader or if anyone is leading you, be encouraged by reading *Staying Fresh*. Packed with personal insights and ministry experience, this book offers an incisive health check for today's leaders. Our spiritual, mental, physical and emotional health is examined by a careful unpacking of God's Word, with a view to sustaining the Christian life until we cross the finishing line. *Staying Fresh* will warm your heart, stretch your mind and strengthen your wobbly knees!

Revd Dr Simon Vibert, Vice Principal, Director of the School of Preaching, Wycliffe Hall

STAYING FRESH

PAUL MALLARD

STAYING FRESH

SERVING WITH JOY

ivp

INTER-VARSITY PRESS
Norton Street, Nottingham NG7 3HR, England
Email: ivp@ivpbooks.com
Website: www.ivpbooks.com

British Library Cataloguing in Publication Data
A catalogue record for this book is available from the British Library.

ISBN: 978-1-78359-193-0

Set in Dante 11.5/14pt
Typeset in Great Britain by CRB Associates, Potterhanworth, Lincolnshire
Printed in Great Britain by Ashford Colour Press Ltd, Gosport, Hampshire

*Inter-Varsity Press publishes Christian books that are true to the Bible and that
communicate the gospel, develop discipleship and strengthen the church for its mission
in the world.*

*Inter-Varsity Press is closely linked with the Universities and Colleges Christian
Fellowship, a student movement connecting Christian Unions in universities and colleges
throughout Great Britain, and a member movement of the International Fellowship of
Evangelical Students. Website: www.uccf.org.uk*

Contents

To Les Coley –
pastor and preacher,
and Peter Barham –
friend and co-worker

Preface

As I look back over more than thirty years of leading local churches as well as serving groups of churches scattered across the United Kingdom, I have come to some firm convictions about Christian leadership. Healthy and growing churches are almost always led by bold, faithful and visionary leaders. When there is an absence of leadership, there will always be a negative effect on the health of the church. Leadership is not a dirty word; it is a God-designed and God-given means of blessing his people.

The health of the church depends on the health of its leaders.

Spiritually vital leadership will lead to a spiritually vital church. Leaders whose lives are marked out by holiness and love may not lead large and fashionable churches, but they will lead healthy and faithful ones. There's nothing wrong with wanting to see numerical growth – in fact there is something perverse about being content when people are not being added to the church. However, our deepest concern should be for the spiritual temperature of the church, and this is intimately related to the spiritual temperature of its leaders.

Why not read this book with your fellow leaders? If you are a husband, you might find it helpful to consider some of the questions with your wife. Or read it with a more mature Christian leader who can invest some time in your life. And even if you are not a leader and never aspire to be one, why not use this book as a personal spiritual health check?

We need better leaders if we are to meet the challenges of the days in which we live. And leadership always has to begin with a consideration of character and spiritual vitality.

There is no short cut to spiritual vitality and this book cannot promise one. We serve a God who is gracious and generous and who takes us from where he finds us and transforms us to make us like Christ. Let's explore how God works with us to enable us to lead faithful churches that glorify his name and accomplish his purposes. Are you ready for the challenge?

Paul Mallard

Foreword

Social commentators tell us that across the Western world there is a crisis of leadership. There are many contributory factors, but they include the pressurized nature of the role and the ever-present media intrusion. The whole of life seems to be swallowed up by the weight of responsibility, and the whole of life, public and private, is under constant scrutiny.

When we come to leadership within the Christian community, the situation is not dissimilar, for a leadership crisis is evident in many churches too. In the UK and North America, Christian ministers often struggle to serve more than a decade (maybe much less) before buckling under the pressure. In response, there is also evidence of some professionalization of ministry, which distances leaders from true community and attempts to keep public and private lives separate. And it is becoming harder to recruit leaders across the spectrum – for home groups, for work with children and youth, and for other leadership roles within the church.

Paul Mallard has written for a wide audience and for leaders of all kinds, whether they influence a congregation or a small group of just two or three, and his book is a hugely welcome contribution to defining healthy Christian leadership at all levels. Reminding us of Paul's exhortation to Timothy to 'watch your life and doctrine closely' (1 Timothy 4:16), Paul Mallard has no doubts about the importance of right doctrine. But his book addresses the urgent need of *watching your life*, and does so with a refreshing candour, humour and directness.

Reading these chapters, we discover some unexpected words and concepts for leaders, such as *joy, holiness, humanity, accountability, mortification, dependence, recreation* and much else. But what strikes me as the overriding quality of Paul Mallard's writing – and, indeed, his own example – is the emphasis on relational strength. That is, he urges us to see that the secret of godly leadership – joyful and sustainable leadership – rests in strong relationships. These include our nurtured and growing relationship with God himself; our committed and loving relationships with spouse and family and friends; our servant and sacrificial relationship with those to whom we minister; and our wise and realistic relationship with our own spiritual, moral and physical well-being.

Whatever sphere of Christian service in which we are engaged, the following pages are sure to strengthen our love for the Lord and our love for people – the very things which Jesus said mattered most.

Jonathan Lamb
CEO and minister-at-large, Keswick Ministries
Oxford, UK

Introduction

Beware of garden equipment

It is a Thursday night in high summer. After a hard day's teaching, I arrive home and have a couple of hours to spare before an important church meeting.

In pensive mood I go into the garden to do some digging. Is my mind elsewhere? Perhaps. I have only been turning the earth for a few minutes when I lift the fork and plunge it into my foot. Accidentally of course.

My boot fills with blood and my face drains of colour. When I remove the boot, I find a lovely neat hole right through the centre of my left foot. I limp to the house, and my wife insists that I need to go to A & E. She sweeps up our baby son and runs next door to deposit him with a kind neighbour.

Then she drives me to the hospital. It seems very busy and I muse whether or not there are any other distracted gardeners here tonight. My wife is not amused.

After a long wait, I finally hobble to a cubicle. They prod and probe. They inject and stitch. They bandage and bind.

In short, they keep me late and I miss the meeting. And my life is changed forever.

God moves in a mysterious way

I became a Christian when I was eleven years old. By the age of fourteen, I had a strong inner conviction that God wanted me to be engaged in some form of full-time Christian ministry. I had little idea of what that meant and even less idea about how to pursue it.

So a couple of years later I asked one of the church leaders what I should do. 'Get a proper job first,' he gruffly advised. So that was what I did. I studied theology and became an RE teacher. I got married. My wife shared my convictions about full-time Christian service. We joined a small church in Chippenham, and God blessed us with a son.

The church asked me to serve as part of its leadership team, and I began to develop as a preacher and get involved in pastoral care. Over the next two years the church began to grow and became convinced that it needed to call a full-time pastor.

I was acting as church secretary at the time, and so it was I who prepared the agenda for the church members' meeting where we would discuss the calling of a minister.

This was the night when I suffered my unfortunate gardening accident. And having missed the meeting, I was keen to find out what had been decided. I didn't have to wait long. Shortly after breakfast the next day, I had a 'pastoral visit' from two of my fellow elders. They showed concern about my self-inflicted injury and then got down to business.

'We had the meeting last night,' they said. 'Sorry you couldn't be there, but it meant that we were free to discuss you! We came to two conclusions: we want a pastor, and we want you to be that pastor. Is that OK?'

Six months later I was ordained as the pastor of that church. My wife and I enjoyed thirteen and a half happy and fruitful years serving people we already knew and loved.

I think I learned two lessons.

Firstly, be careful of garden equipment, especially if your mind is elsewhere!

Secondly, God moves in a mysterious way his wonders to perform.[1] God's call to service is unique and tailor-made for each of us. It usually involves a combination of biblical conviction (guidance from the Bible), circumstantial direction (guidance from circumstances) and public recognition (affirmation from fellow believers).

At the time of writing I have been involved in Christian leadership for over thirty years. This has been in the context of three local churches as well as a partnership of churches. One of the greatest encouragements I have enjoyed is being involved in training other leaders. I have also had the privilege of pastoring pastors.

What lessons have I learned along the way?

The man after God's own heart

Certain essential ingredients are vital for successful Christian leadership.

Psalm 78:70–72 describes the choosing and leadership of King David:

> He [God] chose David his servant
>   and took him from the sheepfolds;
> from tending the sheep he brought him
>   to be the shepherd of his people Jacob,
>   of Israel his inheritance.
> And David shepherded them with integrity of heart;
>   with skilful hands he led them.
> (78:70–72)

David was God's choice and God's gift. He was both the servant of the Lord and the shepherd of his flock. The skills he learned as a shepherd prepared him well for shepherding the nation.

What qualified him to do this? Three things:

Conviction

David knew that he had been called and chosen by God. His first recorded words show that he was a man of passionate faith (1 Samuel 17:26, 45–47). Leaders must be people of deep conviction who have an abiding confidence in God.

Competence

He led the people with 'skilful hands'. He had the gifts necessary to lead people in the right direction. He was able to unite a divided nation, overcome their enemies and lead them to a place of peace and prosperity (2 Samuel 7:1).

Character

David shepherded the people with 'integrity of heart'. He was the kind of man that God could trust. He was honest and upright, truthful and reliable. He led well because his heart was right.

Learning from David

These three attributes continue to be essential for any form of Christian leadership today.

Conviction is vital. A postmodern world is suspicious of absolute truth and passionate conviction. Yet leaders must be driven by clear theological commitments and the knowledge that God is calling them to make a difference. Leadership is about tackling issues and instituting change. A leader wants to make a difference because his convictions make a difference. Without conviction, leadership falters and fails. Why would you want to lead if you have no sense of direction? Why would people want to follow you?

Competence is essential. Some leaders have settled convictions and are good and godly people, but they lack the necessary skills to give the kind of vision and direction that are needed. Their lack of competence leads to frustration among those whom they are seeking to lead. They may make a healthy contribution to a wider leadership team, but on their own they can be a disaster.

Character is indispensable. An absence of conviction and competence among leaders will damage the cause of Christ. But this is nothing compared to a lack of integrity. History is strewn with the tragic record of those who have injured the church and impaired its witness through their private sins and public misdemeanours. There have been leaders who were astonishingly gifted and staggeringly charismatic, but whose fatally flawed characters led them into disaster. Churches can actually flourish under such leadership for some time. People become Christians. The preaching is great. The work expands. The leader's sin is hidden. However, it will all end in tears. That's why Paul tells Timothy to watch his life and his doctrine closely (1 Timothy 4:16). Take stock. Take care. If you think you are standing, be careful or you might fall (1 Corinthians 10:12). This is why staying fresh is so important.

Stay fresh

This book will touch on the importance of conviction and competence. But the real emphasis will be on character. It is about persevering in integrity of character so that we do not ruin our reputation or damage the church. It is about persevering in prayer and in discipleship. It is about the determination not to give up in our battle with sin and our service for Christ. It is about being steadfast and persistent when we feel like giving up.

This book is also about staying fresh and joyful in our service.

Integrity of character flows out of intimacy of fellowship. How do we maintain an intimate relationship with God in a busy world? How do we read the Bible to feed our souls rather than 'professionally', looking for the next talk we have to deliver? How do we care for ourselves and avoid either burn-out or 'rust-out'?

I think that losing our freshness and vibrancy is a particular danger for leaders. It is our greatest occupational hazard and it can be a danger at any and every level of leadership – from the pastor to the home-group leader, from the youth worker to the church administrator.

However, the danger of drift is common to all Christians. Even if you are not a leader and never aspire to be one, I hope that what you learn here may help you to maintain the freshness of young love and to encourage others to do so.

So it is with the freshness of young love that we will begin.

Questions

1. How can you know that God has called you to be involved in Christian leadership?
2. How did David's experience as a shepherd prepare him to shepherd God's people?
3. What are the convictions that should characterize a Christian leader?
4. Why are 'skilled hands' necessary for Christian leadership?
5. Why is character the most important qualification for Christian leadership?

1. When love turns cold

Young love is a wonderful thing.

The first time they meet, there is an unmistakable chemistry and unexpected pyrotechnics. Is there such a thing as love at first sight? They would certainly say so!

As the relationship blossoms, their love deepens. He enters the room, and her heart misses a beat. She brushes the back of his hand, and he is filled with wonder. Hours seem like minutes as they hold hands and enjoy the silence. With her he does not have to pretend – she can see behind the mask he sometimes wears and loves him for who he really is. For her, there is the discovery of the absolute security of knowing that someone really loves her without condition or degree. He sees her face everywhere; she hears his voice on the wind. Such love can spin gold from straw.

Friends watch with mild amusement. When the engagement is announced, they nod their heads sagely. Marriage is always difficult – like dancing in a minefield – but if ever there was a marriage that was bound for bliss, it is this one.

The first few months seem to confirm that this love will endure. Neither of them can wait to get home in the evening. Weekends are like little tastes of Paradise. The honeymoon stretches on and on. Friends wish they could find a treasure like this.

And then it begins to change.

It is almost imperceptible at first. And there is certainly no change on his part. He feels the same passion as ever, but he begins to notice little things. She does not text him quite so many times during the day. When he smiles at her, her face does not light up like it used to. She is not so eager to share the insignificant details of her life as she once was.

As time goes by, the almost imperceptible becomes the glaringly obvious. She always seems to find an excuse to work late. She returns his 'I love you', but it seems to lack conviction. He catches a pained expression when she looks at him – she denies it, but he knows what he has seen.

Of course he suspects the worst. There must be someone else. He doesn't want to believe it – it can't be true surely. But what other explanation can there be?

He dreads the confrontation and keeps putting it off. There are moments when things seem to be as they were, and so he holds on. But in the end he can't stand it any longer.

They sit facing each other. With a dry mouth and a beating heart, he begins to pick away at the scab that their relationship has become. At first she is evasive. She is angry in her denials and aggressive in her counter-accusations. But then everything seems to change. Like a great mountain of ice, she melts before him:

'I have been dreading this – I knew it was coming, but I wanted to avoid it. I don't want to hurt you. Yet there is no-one else. There never has been. There never will be. I take my vows seriously. I will never desert you, and as far as it is possible I will always play the role of a good wife. It's just that I don't love you like I used to. The feeling has gone. I don't know how or why, but I cannot get it back. I don't think I will ever feel the way I did. I'm so sorry. I know how much this must hurt you. Please forgive me. I just don't think that things can ever be as they were.'

How does he feel? Is he relieved? Is he reassured?

Of course not!

He is devastated. His world has been shattered in a thousand pieces. It feels like the grief of bereavement – and in a way that's exactly what it is. His mind runs through a vista of possibilities. Where did it go wrong? What can he do to win back her heart? It seems so final – is there any hope among the ashes?

Young love is a wonderful thing. And its loss is painful beyond description.

A famous church

Jesus once spoke to a church which had shown passionate love.

The city at Ephesus was one of the greatest cities in the Roman Empire. The Temple of Aphrodite, one of the Seven Wonders of the World, dominated the skyline. It was famous for sorcery and the dark arts. An 'Ephesian letter' described a magic spell that you could purchase in order to curse an enemy or captivate a lover.

The church in Ephesus enjoyed a pedigree next to none. Paul had planted it around AD 52 (Acts 19:1–40), and it became a hub from which other churches were planted. On his way to Jerusalem, Paul made a point of calling the elders of Ephesus to meet him, to warn them about the challenges and encouragements of ministry (Acts 20:7–38). Paul's letter to the Ephesians has been described as the crown of his theology. Timothy served as one of the church's first pastors (1 Timothy 1:3), and the apostle John retired there. It is said that when John was too frail to walk, the young men of the church would carry him in among God's people, and when they requested a sermon, he would pull himself up on his pallet and simply repeat the profound and powerful words: 'Little children, love one another.'[1]

In those early days the church was marked by a passionate love for Jesus. Many were converted, and the magicians burned their books (Acts 19:17–19). Later they were willing to suffer persecution because of their love for Christ (Acts 19:21–40). Paul's last words to the church pick up on this love for Jesus: 'Grace to all who love our Lord Jesus Christ with an undying love' (Ephesians 6:24).

A passionate Saviour

By the end of the first century, the New Testament church was over sixty years old. John had been arrested and imprisoned on the island of Patmos – a penal colony off the coast of Turkey. He is in the Spirit on the Lord's Day, and suddenly the Christ, the Lord of glory, appears to him. This is not the 'gentle Jesus meek and mild' of popular imagination. Nor is it the victim of Calvary stained with blood and disfigured beyond measure. This is Jesus as he is now, the conqueror of death and the King of heaven.

John hears the voice and turns to see the vision. The images John uses to describe this vision build up a picture of overwhelming majesty and awe-inspiring magnificence (Revelation 1:9–20). Christ's face shines like the sun in all its glory, and John cannot bear it. The 'beloved disciple' who once sat close to his Lord at the Last Supper now falls at his feet as if he is dead.

With amazing tenderness and gentleness, Jesus stoops and lifts John from the dust and sets him on his feet. He has appeared to John because he wants to speak to the churches of Asia Minor. He wants to comfort and challenge them. He wants to shine a light into the dark and hidden places of their lives so that they will be transformed and become what they were meant to be.

An evaluation

And first on the list is the church in Ephesus. Did John's heart skip a beat when he heard the name of the church he had served so faithfully for many years? Was he surprised by what he heard?

The Lord of the church is actively and immediately and intimately present in his church (Revelation 2:1). What does he see? Forget reputation or appearance or history – all that really matters is Christ's own evaluation.

There is much to applaud, and Jesus is not grudging in his praise.

It is a busy church. 'I know your deeds, your hard work and your perseverance' (2:2). This church has a demanding programme and a full notice sheet. Christianity is not a spectator sport, and in any healthy church there will be an abundance of gospel-driven activity. It's good to be busy in the service of Jesus.

It is a theologically discerning church. Some churches are naïve about truth. Not so Ephesus. They have tested the false apostles who have turned up, and have rejected their message (2:2). They hate the destructive effects of the false teaching associated with a group known as the 'Nicolaitans' (2:6). The health of the church depends on its loyalty to the truth. Ephesus is loyal.

It is a faithful church. 'You have persevered and have endured hardships for my name, and have not grown weary' (2:3). In a world in which there is a growing antipathy to Christian values, and in which being a Christian is becoming increasingly dangerous, they do not compromise or hold back. They are willing to suffer for their faith.

The Lover's voice

So much to commend – this is just the kind of church you would want to join. We can tick most of the boxes. If your kids rang from university to tell you that they had decided to join this church, you would be chuffed!

Surely there is nothing more to say.

Unfortunately, there is something that may be invisible to us, but is glaringly obvious to Jesus: 'Yet I hold this against you: you have forsaken the love you had at first' (2:4).

'You do not love me like you used to. You have grown cold. Your passion has cooled.' The word used for 'forsaken' has the idea of desertion or neglect. It is used of the disciples when they deserted Jesus and fled from his side in the Garden of Gethsemane (Mark 14:50).

To a casual observer, they are all that a church should be, but Jesus sees beneath the surface and knows the true state of their hearts. They are diligent in their religion, but distant in their relationship.

And these are not the words of an enraged Master, but of a tender-hearted Lover. Christ is the passionate Saviour of his church who gave everything to purchase her salvation. In the words of the hymn:

> From heaven he came and sought her
> to be his holy bride.
> With his own blood he bought her,
> and for her life he died.[2]

Like the young woman in the story earlier, the church at Ephesus might respond, 'There is no-one else. There never has been. There never will be. I take my vows seriously . . . It's just that I don't love you like I used to . . . I'm so sorry. I know how much this must hurt you. Please forgive me. I just don't think that things can ever be as they were.'

Is that enough for Jesus? Of course not! A duty love and duty service are not sufficient for a Saviour who has loved his people extravagantly and without measure.

This is serious

And this not a negligible or an insignificant matter:

Consider how far you have fallen! Repent and do the things you
did at first. If you do not repent, I will come to you and remove
your lampstand from its place.
(2:5)

A church that has lost its first love has no long-term future. It
has lost its way. It has slipped its moorings. It may be busy and
sound and faithful, but if its heart is icy and its passion has
cooled, it is on a journey to oblivion.

To avoid this, the Christians at Ephesus must remember and
repent and return (2:5). They do not need a new experience or
a new teaching or a new programme. They need to go back
to Jesus, to return to where it all started. They need to fly to
the cross.

Jesus' last word is a word of hope (2:7). It's not too late. Those
who come to him will experience the eternal joy of feeding on
the tree of life in the Paradise of
God. In the Bible, life is always
inseparable from fellowship with *A church that has lost*
God. Heaven is the eternal enjoy- *its first love has no*
ment of God experienced in the *long-term future.*
blaze of his glory and the delight
of his love. It is like the experi-
ence of young love over and over and over again. Such love never
disappoints or pales or dies. Instead, throughout all eternity, it
will deepen and mature and grow and never lose its first bloom.

The danger of drift

It's not only churches that can lose the freshness of young love;
this can happen to individuals as well.

I have been a Christian for over forty-five years. As I said
earlier, for more than thirty years I have been engaged in full-time
Christian ministry. I heard the gospel of God's grace for the first

time when I was seven through the work of a summer holiday club for children. I came to Christ at the age of eleven. Don't ever let anyone tell you that a child cannot understand that he/she needs Jesus. When I fled to the cross for forgiveness, it was not a nice little middle-class decision. I knew I needed Christ. The old hymn puts it perfectly:

> Nothing in my hand I bring,
> Simply to Thy cross I cling;
> Naked, come to Thee for dress;
> Helpless, look to Thee for grace;
> Foul, I to the fountain fly;
> Wash me, Saviour, or I die.[3]

At that moment I loved Jesus more than words can tell. If someone had said that now that I was a Christian, I had to sail to China as a missionary, I would not have thought it was too much to ask. On the wall of the room where our youth group met hung a poster with the famous words of C. T. Studd: 'If Jesus Christ be God and died for me, then no sacrifice can be too great for me to make for Him.' It seemed entirely reasonable.

The warm glow soon faded, but it was replaced by a deep and intense desire to follow Jesus. It doesn't sound very sophisticated, but I loved Jesus and didn't care who knew it. My first attempts at evangelism were clumsy and probably too intense, but being cool didn't figure in the vocabulary of my spirituality. When I went off to study theology at Cambridge, I covered my cases, duffel coat and books with those garish fluorescent stickers you could buy in the 1970s. In gaudy letters they announced, 'Smile, God loves you' or 'Prepare to meet your God.' I looked like a walking Belisha beacon. What a wally! As I look back, I blush to think about it, but at the time I just wanted people to know how much I loved my Saviour.

Today I am slightly more sophisticated and rather less demonstrative. However, as I remember those early days, I often wish

I could regain that first flush of passion. I look back over my ministry and am aware that there have been times when outwardly I have appeared to be a healthy and vibrant follower of Jesus, but my heart has felt like a lead weight. Praying has been an exercise in repetition without reality. I have read the Bible out of a sense of duty rather than with any expectation of joy. Yes, I still followed Jesus and said that I loved him. Sometimes I even preached about him, but with a passion that I did not feel. No-one would have suspected a thing – but I knew. Lovers long to be alone, and I had no hunger or desire to be with Jesus.

How can I confess these things and maintain any credibility as a Christian leader?

For two reasons.

Firstly, I stand in the grace of God. The only confidence I can ever have is based on the kindness and mercy of God's heart. He saved me by grace alone; he keeps me by grace alone; I remain in ministry by grace alone.

Secondly, I suspect that my experience is not unique. The struggle to avoid drifting away from an intimate relationship with God is almost overwhelming. Life is just so busy, and we are crushed by its multiple demands. Sometimes sorrow sweeps over us and numbs our emotions so that it feels as if it is always winter and never Christmas. Sometimes we just wake up and realize that our love for Christ is not what it once was.

Maintain your first love

Of course we will all express our love for Christ in different ways. Some people are demonstrative by nature – they find it easy to be extravagant and outwardly affectionate. Others are more reserved and express their emotions differently. Feelings can be deceptive, and warm words may mask a cold heart. God wants us to be ourselves. We should not feel guilty if we are

Edititofftouredit

temperamentally less effusive than the next person. Nonetheless, the question remains: do we love Christ as we once did?

Duty is not a dirty word, and sometimes we are to do the right thing just because it is the right thing. But duty in itself is not enough. The husband in the opening story could never be satisfied with a wife who 'will always play the role of a good wife', but would never love him as she once did. Jesus could never be satisfied with a church that was busy and sound and faithful, but which had forsaken its first love. In those periods of ministry when I drifted away from an intimate walk with Christ, I knew deep down inside that something was missing and I longed to have it back.

If we are to sustain our service and not become jaded, we need to guard our relationship with God. This is the only way to avoid a creeping cynicism or a stifling professionalism that will slowly erode our effectiveness as servants of God. It needs to become a high priority and an essential ingredient of our daily lives. We can never simply assume that things are well in our relationship with God. We must make a conscious effort to stay fresh.

So where do we start?

Ironically, we start not with our love for Christ but with his love for us.

Questions: What are the signs that my love is growing cold?

1. Lovers love to be alone. Do you look forward to your times of prayer? Do you finish these times feeling refreshed and reinvigorated? Do you read the Bible for ministry or to feed your soul? How is your worship?

2. Healthy Christians are amazed by God's grace. Are you amazed? Does it move you when you remember that Jesus died to save you? Or do you find yourself feeling that God owes you something?

3. If you love Jesus, you will love his people. Do you get angry with individuals who seem to waste your time? Do you get frustrated or cynical about the church?

4. Jesus was the friend of sinners. If you are close to him, you will love what he loves. Do you have a passion for lost people?

5. If we love Jesus, we will want to please him. Are you blasé about sin? Do you hate sin because of the feeling of shame that it brings, or because it grieves Jesus?

2. Know that we are loved

He stumbled into my study looking as if the weight of the world was upon his shoulders.

For most of my ministry I have kept Wednesday mornings free so that anyone who wants pastoral help can drop in. People come to seek advice, ask for prayer or just to share the joys and sorrows that occasionally invade our lives. They don't need an appointment – they just turn up, and I help if I can.

He was there very early and he looked as if he hadn't slept. Anxiety was written all over his face.

Before I could ask, he blurted it out: 'Pastor, you have got to help me. I don't know what to do. I've just had my first argument with my wife.'

They had been married for six months. I was amazed that it had taken them so long!

Mustering my most concerned expression, I asked him to tell me what had happened. He did – it was something about washing up, if I remember correctly. It was no big deal. As far as I could tell, there was no underlying problem. The cause of his concern was really the fact that they had never argued before.

This was unexplored territory, and he didn't know the way back to base camp.

I could have given him some deeply spiritual advice, drawing out the theological implications of trying to build relationships in a world marred by sin. Instead, I went for the easy option: 'Go home. On the way, buy her some flowers. Give them to her, and tell her you love her and you are sorry and you want to put things right. I guarantee that everything will be fine.'

He was assured and left with a new spring in his step. I felt the warm glow that comes from knowing that at least one pastoral problem has been easily solved.

I saw him again on Sunday. 'How did it go?' I asked.

'It was a disaster. I gave her the flowers, and she threw them at me!' he said.

This was a bit of a shock, so I asked him to tell me exactly what he had done.

'I did exactly what you told me to do. I stopped at the garage on the way home and bought the second-cheapest bunch of flowers. But they weren't grotty or anything – they were quite nice. Then I went home and told her what you had said: "The pastor told me to tell you that I love you . . ."'

We live and learn!

What we all need to know

We all need to know that we are loved.

Husbands need to tell their wives, and wives need to tell their husbands. Parents need to tell their children, and children need to tell their parents. Pastors need to tell their congregations, and congregations need to tell their pastors.

This is neither a luxury nor an indulgence. We need to know we are loved because we have been made in the image of God, and God is love. Indeed, the most fundamental and breathtaking truth about God is that he exists eternally in an unclouded and perfect relationship of mutual love and boundless adoration. The Father has always loved the Son; the Son has always been the darling of the Father's heart. The Holy Spirit is eternally bound up in this celebration of passionate devotion. God has never been lonely. He has never needed to seek another object of affection. The creation of human beings was not a necessity, but a free and sovereign choice flowing out of this eternal and unquenchable love.

Since we are imprinted with the image of this God, it naturally follows that the most important things in our lives are relationships. We are created to love God by enjoying him and glorifying him forever. This is our ultimate calling as human beings and the particular purpose of our Christian discipleship. Knowing God is more important than serving him, and loving him is more fundamental than achieving things in his name.

The Shepherd's heart

What has this got to do with leadership?

Everything.

As we saw in the Lord's words to the church at Ephesus, Jesus is looking for the loving devotion of our hearts. This is more important than activism or doctrinal correctness or courage in the face of suffering. We should never despise these things, but they are no substitute for a warm loving relationship. And this applies particularly to Christian leadership. Our service must flow from our devotion. Our ministry is to be ignited by our love. Our activity must stream from hearts captivated by the grace of God.

But how do we cultivate such love? Where do we find it when ministry seems hard and people seem unresponsive? How do we keep it warm when we have to do painful things and when disappointments flood in? We had such high hopes and such great ideals when we started, but we now feel ground down and disillusioned. Our best plans are thwarted, and our highest hopes are frustrated.

And then we are told that we are supposed to love God with a heart that is overflowing with gratitude. Isn't this asking too much? Why not just stiffen the sinews and summon up the blood and cast myself into the breach one last time? Isn't it enough that I am doing my duty? Surely God cannot expect any more?

But that is surely the point.

Do you remember how Jesus reinstates Peter after his terrible lapse of loyalty? (John 21:15–17). Three times he asks Peter the same question: 'Do you love me?' Peter denies his Lord three times – and Jesus gives him three opportunities to reaffirm his love. Three times Peter answers in the affirmative, and each time Jesus tells him to care for his flock.

The essential qualification of a shepherd is that he loves Jesus, and so loves his flock. That is why Jesus asks Peter the question three times. You cannot do a shepherd's job without a shepherd's heart. And you will never have a shepherd's heart unless first of all you love the chief Shepherd.

The key that unlocks love

We cannot 'will' this kind of love. We cannot work ourselves up and decide to demonstrate it just because the pastor told us to do it.

So what is the key that unlocks such love? Ironically, it is where we started. It is in knowing that we are loved. The more we are overwhelmed by God's love, the more we will find a responsive instinct of love rising in our hearts. We will come to love as we are loved.

So where does leadership begin? Where does it need to return to? Where does it flourish, and where does it find the strength to endure? Where does it stay fresh and remain healthy? The answer is the same in every case: it is in the contemplation of

God's great love for us, planned in eternity, promised in history, personified in Jesus and poured out at Calvary. As we gaze at this love, as we dwell in the shadow of the cross, as we realize that he is dying as our substitute and as we stand amazed in the presence of Jesus the Nazarene, we will find the resources we need for the journey. What is more, we will find that we do love what he loves and long for the things that please his heart.

Knowing that God loves us is so important that it forms the substance of one of Paul's greatest prayers.

Paul's prayer about grasping love

Paul wanted the Christians in Ephesus to grasp the greatness of God's love for them:

> For this reason I kneel before the Father, from whom every family in heaven and on earth derives its name. I pray that out of his glorious riches he may strengthen you with power through his Spirit in your inner being, so that Christ may dwell in your hearts through faith. And I pray that you, being rooted and established in love, may have power, together with all the Lord's holy people, to grasp how wide and long and high and deep is the love of Christ, and to know this love that surpasses knowledge – that you may be filled to the measure of all the fullness of God. (Ephesians 3:14–19)

The substance of this prayer is very simple: God loves you more than you can imagine, and he wants you to know it. God really does want us to know this. He wants us to rejoice in it, to bask in its warm glow and to celebrate its boundless immensity. This is not self-indulgence or an unnecessary luxury reserved for the élite of the elect. It is the will and purpose of God. The great Puritan theologian John Owen grasped this in the seventeenth century: 'The greatest sorrow and burden you can lay on the

Father, the greatest unkindness you can do him, is not to believe that he loves you.'[1]

A solid foundation

Paul prays to the Father that he might strengthen the Christians by the Spirit so that they may be filled with the fullness of the Son (3:14–17). Paul's motive for his prayer is that they may be 'rooted and established in love' (3:17).

There are two images here.

Firstly, Paul wants their lives to resemble a tree with its roots sunk deeply into the refreshing soil of God's love. Picture a mighty oak or a majestic pine. It stands firmly in spite of time and change. Its roots, most of which are unseen, give it stability and strength, health and fruitfulness. This is a common biblical image:

> But blessed is the one who trusts in the LORD,
>   whose confidence is in him.
> They will be like a tree planted by the water
>   that sends out its roots by the stream.
> It does not fear when heat comes;
>   its leaves are always green.
> It has no worries in a year of drought
>   and never fails to bear fruit.
> (Jeremiah 17:7–8)

The second picture is of a building established on solid foundations. The most important part of any man-made structure is the part you cannot see: the foundations that give it support and solidity. So if you want to build high, you have to go deep. We are reminded of Jesus' parable of the two builders (Matthew 7:24–27). We are all builders, and every building has a foundation, and all foundations are tested, but only one foundation will stand.

Like a tree caught in a storm or impacted by drought, we face a thousand natural shocks. Like a building, we find ourselves rocked by the earthquake of adverse circumstances. When this happens, we need to know that our roots are deep and our foundations are secure.

What is the soil in which we must be rooted? What is the foundation on which we must build? It is the love of God for his children. Our love for him is often fickle and vacillating. His love for us by contrast is constant and resolute. It was demonstrated at Calvary and inscribed on our hearts by the Holy Spirit. He wants us to have a deep and solid assurance that he loves us unconditionally and will never cease to act for our good.

Life is painful. Leadership is costly. Those whom we trusted sometimes malign us. We invest time and tears in people who go on to break our hearts. We work so hard and see so little fruit. What do we need to know? If we are joyfully to endure, we must continue to trust that even in these circumstances, God has not stopped loving us. When we fail and feel useless and condemned, we need to remember that God has not stopped loving us.

So often we are self-obsessed, trying to gauge and measure the tepid responses of our hearts. It is right to examine our hearts, and self-knowledge is a biblical imperative. But this can easily become unhealthy introspection. If we are to endure and joyfully continue in our labour for the Lord (1 Corinthians 15:58), then we need to focus on his love, not ours. This contemplation of God's love is what Paul prays for. It will give stability and security in life and leadership.

A staggering description
To help them in their contemplation, Paul now tries to describe this love. He wants the believers to

> have power, together with all the Lord's holy people, to grasp
> how wide and long and high and deep is the love of Christ,
> and to know this love that surpasses knowledge . . .

Paul is not content with a superficial understanding of God's love – he wants them to 'grasp' its greatness. He longs for them to have a firm grip of, and deep insight into, this love.

To capture their imaginations, he raids the vocabulary of dimensional adjectives – God's love is wide and long and high and deep. This love is immeasurable. We are not pressing the text too far if we try to put flesh on the bones of Paul's description.

How wide is God's love? It crosses all barriers – time and history and space. It finds its resting place on every continent and in all cultures. It reaches out to all kinds of people, irrespective of race or sex or age or social standing. It calls into existence a multinational rainbow people of God. It is even so wide that it can encompass people like you and me!

How long is God's love? It is eternal. What was God doing before he created the world? The Father loved the Son with a boundless, limitless, endless love. But there is more to it than that. In eternity he set his love on us. We were chosen in Christ before the foundation of the world (Ephesians 1:4). If an angel could fly back through history exploring the genesis of the divine passion, he would wing his way back beyond the moment you first came to faith, beyond your childhood and birth, past the great events of recorded history, past the cross of Christ and the fall of Adam, beyond the moment of creation. It is only when our angelic investigator arrives in the eternity that is before time, when only the triune God existed, that he will discover the origin of the love God has for us.

How high is God's love? It is so high that it raises sinners up from the depth of their failure and sin and seats them with Christ in the heavenly realms. It blesses them with every spiritual blessing in Christ. Those who come to taste it are ransomed, healed, restored and forgiven. They are transported from the 'guttermost to the uttermost'.

And how deep is this love? It is as deep as Calvary. The greatest distance in the universe is not from one end of the cosmos to another – it is the distance between the throne of heaven and the cross of Calvary. Without ceasing to be God, the Son of God took human nature, adopted the role of a servant and was obedient even to the point of death. And so that we don't miss the point, Paul adds that it was 'even death on a cross' (Philippians 2:6–8). He is betrayed and beaten, he is despised and tortured, he is mocked and murdered. For the first time ever, he steps into the darkness of God's wrath as he who knew no sin is made a sin offering for us (2 Corinthians 5:21). No wonder we sing:

> Here is love, vast as the ocean,
> Lovingkindness as the flood,
> When the Prince of Life, our Ransom,
> Shed for us His precious blood.
> Who His love will not remember?
> Who can cease to sing His praise?
> He can never be forgotten,
> Throughout Heav'n's eternal days.[2]

And just so that we get the point, Paul reminds us that when we have stretched every sinew of our mind and pushed our sanctified imagination to its limits, we have only just begun to touch the edges of this love, a love which 'surpasses knowledge'. It is wider than you thought and longer than you imagined and higher than you anticipated and deeper than you ever dreamed. You don't deserve it, but it is yours nonetheless, unconditionally and unreservedly. It isn't soft, and it will chasten you if you sin. But it will never let you down and it will never let you go.

Exercises

- What are the Bible verses that speak of God's love for his people? Begin to make a list and use it to fuel your prayer life.

- Consider the words of the song, 'Oh, to see the dawn of the darkest day'.[3] What does this tell us about God's love poured out at the cross?
- Make a list of songs/hymns that focus on the cross. Spend some time meditating on what they teach.
- Make a list of the blessings that flow from the cross.
- Find a sermon online that focuses on God's love for us in Christ, and listen to it, making notes and thinking about the implications for your life.

A stunning outcome

Paul now reaches the climax of his prayer.

As they begin to grasp this love that God has for them, his audience will be filled to all the fullness of God. Paul has already prayed that Christ may dwell in their hearts (3:17). Later he will instruct them to be filled with the Holy Spirit (5:18). But here he is thinking of the fullness of God the Father. Christians are joined to Christ by faith and indwelt by the Spirit in such a way that the life of the triune God is at work within them. This we realize and enjoy as, by the power of the Spirit, we contemplate how much God loves us.

To be filled with his fullness is to be controlled by him as we surrender our lives without reserve or regret. It means being transformed by him so that in every dimension of our existence we affirm his lordship and desire his will. It is to be satisfied with him in such a way that he drives out every idol and every other obsession, so that our hearts are filled with a passion for his glory above everything else.

Every day of our lives we should be in a place where we bask in the unconditional, unquenchable, extravagant love that God has for us. This is no abstract theoretical subject. The New Testament almost always links the love of God with the cross of Christ. We started at the cross, and to the cross we must return constantly. All our service is to be offered in the shadow of the cross. All our teaching must be an echo of the cross. All our leadership must be patterned on the cross. The cross must sanctify all our praying and living and suffering.

And as we gaze at Calvary and consider Christ's love for us, we will find a flame of love ignited on the cold altars of our hearts. We will learn to love Christ, to long for him and to live for him. We will want to enjoy him forever.

It is this joy in the Lord which we will now consider.

Questions

1. Read Psalm 103. What does David tell us about God's love for his people?
2. Read Romans 8:31–39. How does Paul help us to understand God's love in these verses?
3. Why do we doubt God's love for us?
4. What will happen to our Christian service if it does not flow from the contemplation of God's love for us?
5. What is the relationship between love and obedience and duty?

3. Rejoice in the Lord

Try the following exercise.

Write down the ten most important things in your life, the things that define you. What do you spend your time and energy on? What do people associate with you? What makes you tick?

Don't try to put them in any particular order – that comes later.

You may be pushed to find ten things, but keep going. Some things are predictable. Family, friends, health and career usually find a place on most people's list. Other things will be unique to you – books on medieval church history, chess, cross-stitch or West Bromwich Albion Football Club.

Now look at your list.

You have to extract one item. Once your choice is made, that thing is gone forever. Never again will you play chess, breed newts or look through a telescope. Juggling, origami or taxidermy is now a thing of the past. It may feel like a little bereavement, but not much.

But you are not finished yet. You need to repeat the process. This time the choice is between genealogy and skydiving or hiking and herpetoculture. The decision may be harder, but it is still fairly comfortable.

You may have guessed where this is going.

Keep repeating the process until only three things remain. By now, some very significant things have departed into the ether. For most people, what is now left is what really counts – things like family, health or vocation.

Remove one more item from your big three. When I have asked people to try this exercise, they have often baulked at this point. The choice is too personal, too painful, too private. But persist!

You are down to two – your highest priorities. And now it is a straight choice. Which can you afford to lose, and which do you refuse to abandon? Be honest. What is the most important relationship, ambition or possession in your life?

If the last remaining priority is anything other than God – your relationship with Father, Son and Holy Spirit – then your Christian discipleship is in a perilous state of decline and decay, and your leadership is in danger.

A bit harsh?

Does this sound a bit harsh? At first sight it may do, but remember the words of Jesus:

> Large crowds were travelling with Jesus, and turning to them he said: 'If anyone comes to me and does not hate father and mother, wife and children, brothers and sisters – yes, even their own life – such a person cannot be my disciple. And whoever does not carry their cross and follow me cannot be my disciple.'
> (Luke 14:25–27)

These words sound pretty shocking. But we must remember that Jesus is speaking idiomatically. 'Hate' is a Semitic expression for loving less. The Bible teaches that we must love the members of our own family, but we must love God even more. If you are framing your list, then your love for God must be the last thing remaining.

And remember that this is Jesus – the rabbi from Galilee – speaking. He is calling for personal allegiance to himself and a willingness to follow the path of suffering that he is pioneering. No wonder his hearers are up in arms. This is blasphemy!

Except that it isn't, because the one who speaks is none other than God himself.

The deity of Christ is the underlying substratum of the New Testament. It is proclaimed by the apostles and affirmed in their writings. It is the assumption behind the demands that Jesus makes of his followers. If it is not true, then Jesus is at best a deluded fool and at worst a wicked charlatan. But the testimony of the apostles, the continued existence of the church and the personal witness of millions of Christians over 2,000 years is that Jesus is exactly who he claims to be.

Jesus demands absolute allegiance.

This brings us back to our starting point.

Jesus demands absolute allegiance. He will not share first place with any other person, thing or ambition in life. We are to love him with an exclusivity and a passion that defines our existence and controls our lives.

The idol of ministry

Perhaps the gravest error that any leader can make is to fall in love with their ministry and allow it to become a substitute for God. Instead of loving Christ, we begin to love what we do for him. We begin to define ourselves by what we do rather than what we are.

We started so well. When we were invited to lead that Bible study or head up that youth ministry or pastor that group of people, we were thrilled to have the opportunity to serve Jesus. We knew that he had saved us. We loved to read about him and speak well of him. We were so thrilled when we actually got the opportunity to do something for him.

But slowly it changed.

We began to love the job we were doing. Nothing wrong with that. But the affection became more and more central in our lives. We resented criticism and became defensive. We did not want to share our service with anyone else. When we finally had to step down, we felt bitter and empty.

We had forgotten the Master and substituted the ministry.

Am I exaggerating? I think not. I have met this trait in a number of passionate Christian workers. I think of the concerned friend who asked me for advice. He had just begun to pastor a church and discovered that the organist, a man in his late 70s, protected his ministry like a ferocious Rottweiler. After a few months, he made the tentative suggestion that this man might like to share his music ministry and undertake some succession planning. This was met with a frosty silence. Late that night he received an angry phone call from the man's daughter: 'How dare you make such a suggestion? Don't you know how long Dad has been playing? It's what he lives for. If you take it away, it will kill him.'

I wish I could say that this was uncommon. But it isn't. I have come across it in a whole variety of contexts: musicians and Bible teachers, youth specialists and church secretaries, missionaries and crèche supervisors.

Ministry turns into an idol. Of course no-one plans for this – it just happens. Sometimes it is slow and imperceptible – it just creeps up on us. Getting ministry into perspective can be a struggle.

Exercise: What are the signs of ministry idolatry?

Work through this list and honestly examine your heart for any of the following danger signs:

- I neglect prayer and personal devotions – the demands of ministry make me too busy to pray.
- I develop a 'martyr complex' – 'Poor me. No-one understands!'
- I overwork and lose the ability to say no. I justify myself by my labours and need to be needed.
- I am plagued by perfectionism. I am discouraged when my service is less than perfect, and yet I refuse to delegate because no-one else can do it as well as I can.
- I become hypercritical. I ignore the good in others and focus on their faults and failings.
- I become authoritarian and dictatorial. I drive the sheep rather than tenderly leading them. They are there to serve me, rather than for me to serve.
- I become angry and irritable, leading to frustration with people – why don't they just do what I tell them?
- I become overprotective and I guard my ministry at all costs. This is my church or my home group or my department – keep away! This trait may well mask a hidden fear: what if I'm not quite up to the job?
- I become disappointed and disillusioned – things didn't work out as I had hoped, and ministry becomes a drag rather than a joy.
- I fall into cynicism – I've been there and done that and have bought the T-shirt. No-one can tell me anything I don't know already. Other leaders may be excited and enthusiastic, but they will soon learn!
- I become suspicious of other gifted people – what if others come to respect them more than me? I am envious of their successes and accomplishments.

> • I indulge in *Schadenfreude*, pleasure derived from the
> misfortunes of others, especially with those whose
> ministry is similar to my own.

Confession time

I hate to admit it, but there have been times when I have struggled
with many of these negative mindsets. They are the signs of
ownership rather than servanthood. The moment that we begin
to talk about 'my ministry' or 'my church' or 'my people', we
should be careful. We should have a warm and intimate relationship with those we serve, but we need to remember that we
serve them, not the other way round.

Of course leaders must lead. We should not shirk the
responsibility of taking God's people forward. This will involve
unpopular decisions and potential conflicts. The Bible grants
authority to leaders. But it is the authority of the servant. People
do not exist to make us look good or feel successful. If there were
a symbol of Christian leadership, it would not be a crown or
sceptre, not a sword or a management certificate. The symbol
would be a towel. We are called to take the lowest position
and, following Jesus' example, to wash one another's feet
(John 13:3–5, 12–17).

Jesus makes it clear that it is all about service:

A dispute also arose among them as to which of them was
considered to be greatest. Jesus said to them, 'The kings of the
Gentiles lord it over them; and those who exercise authority over
them call themselves Benefactors. But you are not to be like that.
Instead, the greatest among you should be like the youngest, and
the one who rules like the one who serves. For who is greater, the
one who is at the table or the one who serves? Is it not the one
who is at the table? But I am among you as one who serves.'
(Luke 22:24–27)

The sin behind the sin

But behind all this there is a deeper problem – the sin behind the
sin. We 'idolize' our ministry because we have allowed it to
replace Christ as the centre of our affections. It has dethroned
and superseded him. We have traded the love of Christ for the
love of what we do for him. What really excites us is human
acclaim and the 'rush' which we get from a job well done. Our
ministry has become a respectable mistress.

And we may continue to enjoy great successes. Gifts can be
separated from relationship. This was part of the problem that
Paul had to address at Corinth. Here was an incredibly gifted
bunch of individuals. There was no lack of talent in this church.
And it seems to have been successful too. The multitude of
problems which Paul identifies were the problems of life. Lots
of pagans were being converted, and they were bringing with
them their pre-Christian hang-ups.

Paul does not discourage their use of gifts, but warns them
of the danger of ministry without love:

> If I speak in the tongues of men or of angels, but do not have
> love, I am only a resounding gong or a clanging cymbal. If I
> have the gift of prophecy and can fathom all mysteries and all
> knowledge, and if I have a faith that can move mountains, but do
> not have love, I am nothing. If I give all I possess to the poor and
> give over my body to hardship that I may boast, but do not have
> love, I gain nothing.
> (1 Corinthians 13:1–3)

I love preaching. I always have done. It is an amazing privilege
to stand in front of a congregation of God's people and point
them to Christ. I have preached over 3,000 sermons in the last
thirty-five years: my wife says that if you were to put all my
sermons end to end, they still wouldn't reach a conclusion –
which is a bit harsh really!

But here is the danger. There have been times when I have been seduced by the romance of preaching. If I am honest, there have been moments when the exhilaration of exegesis, the pleasure of proclamation and the sheer elation of engaging human beings with the truths of Scripture have been the real delights of my life.

Those of us who preach need to remember that there is nothing wrong with enjoying the glorious honour of preaching Christ. Indeed, we should worry if we don't enjoy it. However, we must never allow it to take the place of Christ.

A few decades ago my wife became seriously ill with a neurological condition, which could have resulted in the end of public ministry for both of us.[1] I remember having to face this as a very real possibility. Amidst the tempest of painful and confusing thoughts that roared through my mind at the time, one of the greatest challenges was the realization that I might never preach again.

It felt like a bereavement.

One morning I dropped the kids off at school and then drove over to Bath where my wife was in hospital. I had several hours in which to be alone with God. That morning I wrestled with the confusing change of circumstances which seemed now to be controlling our future. Among other things, I told God that my church needed me and that it didn't make sense that I was going to have to become a full-time carer. How could the church survive if I was not there?

In a wonderfully patient and tender way, God answered some of my questions that morning. How could the church survive if I wasn't there? A better question was: how did the church survive when I was there?! It survived because it was God's church, not mine – Christ is the chief Shepherd, and I just worked for him.

More than that, the Lord challenged me about my love for him. What was first in my affection? What did I love more: the proclamation of Christ or the Christ I proclaimed? I knew the right answer. I also knew my own heart. After a fierce battle,

I remember sitting on a bench and then getting down onto my knees and praying something like this:

'OK, Lord, I surrender. I want to love you more than my ministry. If you are going to take it from me, then I accept your will. Help me to delight in Jesus. Help me to see that if I have everything but him, then I have nothing. But if I have nothing but him, I have everything.'

There was no immediate sense of relief or joy, but I felt that I had crossed a line.

My ministry did not end. In fact, my wife and I discovered that we were able to minister out of the pain that we felt. And that's another story. But the battle to keep Christ central has never gone away. It is a daily battle. Something in my heart always wants to replace the love of Jesus with the love of the things that I do for him.

You too fight this same battle.

People of joy

What is the answer? What is the secret of victory?

It is to be utterly captivated by the beauty and glory of Jesus.

We need to keep the worship of Christ at the centre of all that we are. Even when ministry is demanding, people are difficult, time is short and life is arduous, we need to maintain our adoration of Christ.

George Müller (1805–98) was a remarkable servant of Jesus. Working out of the city of Bristol, he was both an evangelist and a philanthropist. He founded the Ashley Down orphanage and during his lifetime cared for over 10,000 orphans. He provided an education to the children under his care, establishing 117 schools which offered Christian education to more than 120,000 children. He was a remarkable man of faith and prayer, and the record of his answered prayers is almost unbelievable. His philosophy in life was quite simple:

Faith does not operate in the realm of the possible. There is no glory for God in that which is humanly possible. Faith begins where man's power ends. Be assured, if you walk with Him and look to Him, and expect help from Him, He will never fail you.[2]

In the midst of this incredibly busy life, Müller worked exceedingly hard to maintain a warm relationship with Christ. He wrote these words in his journal:

I saw more clearly than ever that the first great and primary business to which I ought to attend every day was, to have my soul happy in the Lord. How different each day is when the soul is refreshed and made happy early.[3]

Sometimes we have to stop and allow our souls to catch up. If the purpose of ministry is to enable people to see the glory of God, how can we be effective if we ourselves are not delighting in the glory of God?

It may come as a bit of a surprise, but Christians are supposed to be joyful! Joy is not an optional extra which marks out certain kinds of people. If you are not enjoying God, your ministry will be critically impaired. Among a whole host of tensions and pressures, Nehemiah came to confess that the joy of the Lord was his strength (Nehemiah 8:10).

We would see Jesus

Do you adore Christ as you should?

Think of who he is:

He is the theme of the Bible. It's all about him. Jesus made it clear to the two disciples on the road to Emmaus that the Old Testament was about him (Luke 24:25–27, 44–49). He was proclaimed in its feasts and festivals and symbolized in its sacrifices. He was promised in its prophecies and praised in its psalms. He was the Tailor in the garden who prepared clothes for Adam and Eve. He was the heavenly Friend who walked with Enoch and the Angel of the Lord who appeared to Abraham and the Captain of the armies of heaven who met Joshua before the walls of Jericho. And in the New Testament he comes to walk the dusty roads of Israel. He is present in the Gospels and proclaimed in the Epistles and pre-eminent in the book of Revelation. In the Bible we hear his voice and see his face. It is the cradle in which he lies and the chariot in which he rides and the throne on which he sits.

He is the darling of heaven. I used to preach in a little village chapel in Wiltshire. The church secretary retired when he was 100 years old – no slacking there! He would always pray the same prayer in the vestry before the service: 'Thank you for bringing this young man to see us, Lord. And now help him to show us Jesus. Oh, Jesus is so precious to us. He is precious to you, Father. He is the darling of heaven.'

I have never forgotten that phrase. He was the delight of a billion burning seraphim and the source of wonder to countless resplendent angels. But more than that, he was the Darling of the Father's heart. The Father delights in the Son with a peerless, boundless and cloudless joy. And we measure God's love for us by the sacrifice of his beloved Son (John 3:16; 1 John 4:10).

He is the only hope of the world. This world is in rebellion against God, its Creator. It is sophisticated and intelligent and proud, but totally lost. The people we meet every day live in spiritual darkness and die in despair. They are lonely and guilty, and they are going to die. But that is not their most serious problem. Their greatest peril is that they are rebels against a holy and just God. Their sins have offended his perfect standards and made them guilty in his presence. There is nothing they can do to change their circumstances and win acquittal.

And into this situation strides the strong Son of God. He does not offer a new code of ethics or some authenticating experience or a second chance to make things better. He offers himself, and with himself he offers a full and free and total salvation. With Christ come forgiveness and justification and reconciliation and assurance and hope and holiness and heaven. And such a salvation is universally available for all who believe – a hope that will never fade away.

He is the treasure of his people. When we come to know Christ, we discover that he is the treasure beyond price. Look at Paul's short letter to the Philippians. In 104 verses he mentions Jesus over fifty times. What controls his life and expectations? It is Jesus: 'For to me, to live is Christ and to die is gain' (1:21). He insists that Jesus' example should shape the way in which we live (2:5). His ambition in life is to know Jesus, the power of his resurrection and the fellowship of his sufferings (3:10–11). Paul was a Christ-intoxicated man. As we struggle through the battles of an average day, we need constantly to turn our minds to Christ and dwell on the blessings with which he floods our lives. If we have the Son, we have everything.

He is the crucified One. We can never really know Jesus until we know him as the crucified One. All our living and thinking and loving and suffering must be done within earshot of Calvary. Although a stigma and scandal to both first-century and twenty-first-century people, this is the heart of our faith. Here the purpose of God is fulfilled. The cross was not an afterthought, but a plan wrought in eternity. Here the justice of God is demonstrated and the wrath of God is satisfied. Jesus is the substitute for sinners who takes our punishment and pays our debts. Here the love of God is revealed. Here God's enemies are defeated. In apparent weakness, Christ crushes sin and Satan and death. We witness the death of death in the death of Christ.

He is the Lord of the church. We serve in his church, and therefore we serve him. He is the foundation stone of the spiritual building. He is the head of the body. He is the great Shepherd of the flock. He is the Bridegroom who died so that his bride might live. He is the Captain of a spiritual army. He walks among the golden lampstands and knows the condition of the churches more clearly and intimately than we ever could. We should long to meet him in the context of the worship of his people. We should desire to please him above everything else. When we come to his table, we may not be able to see his physical form, but we can rejoice, for

> Amidst us our Belovèd stands,
> And bids us view His piercèd hands;
> Points to the wounded feet and side,
> Blest emblems of the Crucified.[4]

He is at the heart of the hope of his people. Christ rose from the dead and became the Lord of life. One day we will see him as he is now. When that happens, we will become like him, and then forever and ever we will gaze at his glory and sing his praises and delight in his beauty. Eternity will be dominated by the deepening relationship that we enjoy with the triune God: Father, Son and Holy Spirit, through the mediation and merits of Jesus, our Captain and Saviour and King.

As we rejoice in Christ, we find that he becomes the delight of our hearts. This is the only antidote to turning our service for the Lord into a demigod that controls our affections and demands our allegiance.

Rejoicing in Christ also helps us to count the cost and gladly pay the price of ministry.

And to that we will now turn our attention.

Exercises and questions

1. Work through the danger of ministry idolatry signs above and honestly examine your heart.
2. Read through Philippians and make a note of all the references to Christ. What do they tell you about Paul's relationship with Jesus?
3. What is the joy of the Lord? How can we experience it?
4. How does the joy of the Lord help us to guard against idolizing our ministry?

4. Count the cost

I had been a pastor for about three years when our family took a holiday in the beautiful county of Devon. We had two small boys at the time, and this was a much-needed rest.

One day we went looking for a cream tea. If you have ever travelled the Devon roads, you will know that there are places where they meander tortuously. And they are bordered by high and impenetrable hedges which make visibility a real problem. Our boys had started arguing at breakfast and were now continuing their squabble in the back of the car. Slightly distracted, I carefully threaded my way around yet another sharp corner, when suddenly an errant sheep confronted me.

I guess that he had escaped from a nearby field and found his way into the narrow lane right in front of my car. I smashed down on the brake pedal and stopped inches from his nose. The boys stopped fighting. No-one moved. I had always thought that sheep were supposed to be very timid, but he just stood there totally unfazed. There was no way round him. It was like one of those stand-offs that you see in action movies.

Fortunately, my wife was in the car. She is a fount of wisdom and always knows what to do.

'You will have to catch him and return him to the field,' she counselled.

Now I am a Brummie boy. My experience of sheep is severely limited. Up till now, all I knew was that for a good roast dinner, you have to 'slam in the lamb', but that was about it.

I cautiously left the car. Are sheep dangerous? How do you catch them? Tentatively I reached out my hand, and the thing moved away. I took a step nearer, and he took a step back. For the next few minutes we executed what must have looked like a carefully choreographed dance. He anticipated my every move and countered it with his own. All this time my sons were laughing hysterically in the back of the car. My wife, trying very hard not to collapse in uncontrollable hilarity, kept on insisting, 'Don't laugh. He's your dad! Respect him!'

By now I had the measure of the beast, and I managed to catch hold of his fleece. He was filthy. His smell was atrocious. There were small armies of mini-beasts enjoying the hospitality of his warm and welcoming wool. The moment I caught hold of him, many of his passengers decided to transfer residency. I could feel them crawling all over the hands I had plunged into his fleece.

I managed to lift him. The smell grew worse, and I was struck by how heavy and rank this animal was. Labouring under his weight, I shuffled over to the side of the lane. There was a gap in the hedge. With a final effort of will, I lifted him up and threw him through the gap.

He did a gambol and then walked nonchalantly away, without even saying 'thank you'.

That was the day when my respect for shepherds grew exponentially. You have to be pretty tough to be a shepherd. Shepherding is not for wimps.

A tough calling

I remember that the children's Bible which we used with our

kids had a number of pictures of shepherds. They were usually kindly-looking men with freshly blow-dried hair.

That is a million miles from the truth. Ancient shepherds had to be tough blokes who knew how to handle themselves. Sheep are particularly vulnerable creatures. They have no sense of direction and no form of defence. Sheep used to be a form of transferable wealth and were therefore a common target for thieves. They were a ready meal and therefore the prey of ravenous wolves or desperate bears.

The only defence that the sheep has is the shepherd. He stands between the sheep and certain death. Without the shepherd, the sheep is mutton. Shepherds had to develop competency with sling and cudgel. At night they lay protectively across the entrance to the sheep pen: they literally became the gate of the sheep (John 10:7). The shepherd would often have to place himself between the sheep and danger. His life expectancy was correspondingly quite low.

For all this, it was not an honoured or respected profession. Shepherds were often despised and shunned. Theirs was an 'unclean' profession, and they were not welcome in the temple precincts, except as the providers of the regular sacrifices needed for worship. Close proximity to sheep – as my own encounter proved – meant that personal hygiene would be a problem. When a shepherd walked into the room, you knew it without looking.

Shepherding the flock

And yet of all the images that the Bible uses to describe the nature of Christian leadership, the most pervasive one is that of the shepherd. For shepherd, read pastor. The pastor shepherds God's flock.

God himself is the Shepherd of Israel (Psalm 95:7) and the Pastor to all who trust him (Psalm 23:1). He gave his people kings who were to be under-shepherds, leading them in the paths of righteousness. Unfortunately, most of them proved to be worthless shepherds who did not strengthen the weak or heal the sick or bind up the injured (Ezekiel 34:2–6).

In response to this failure, God promises that he will take care of the sheep himself, placing over them a perfect Shepherd from the house of David (Ezekiel 34:11, 23).

This promise is fulfilled in Jesus, the good Shepherd or perfect Pastor (John 10:11–18). In some of the richest words in the whole Bible, Jesus speaks of the tender-hearted love that the good Shepherd has for his flock. He knows them intimately and loves them sacrificially. They know him and trust him and follow him. Through his ministry, they experience life in all its fullness (10:10). Three times he announces the supreme qualification of a shepherd – you recognize him because he lays down his life for the sheep (10:11, 15, 17).

Under-shepherds

Jesus is the good Shepherd, and Christian leaders are called to be 'under-shepherds', acting on his behalf for his vulnerable sheep.

Thus Jesus commissions a newly restored Peter to care for his flock (John 21:15–17), warning him that in the end this will cost him his life (21:18–19). Thirty years later this image is still in Peter's mind. Writing to a group of churches scattered in Asia Minor, he addresses the leaders thus:

> To the elders among you, I appeal as a fellow elder and a witness of Christ's sufferings who also will share in the glory to be revealed: be shepherds of God's flock that is under your care, watching over them – not because you must, but because you are willing, as God wants you to be; not pursuing dishonest gain, but eager to serve; not lording it over those entrusted to you, but being examples to the flock. And when the Chief

Shepherd appears, you will receive the crown of glory that will
never fade away.
(1 Peter 5:1–4)

Jesus is the archetypal Shepherd – the Chief Shepherd. But Christian leaders are called to serve under his direction and guidance.
What an astonishing calling we have: shepherds of God's flock!

We are to be marked by an enthusiasm in service and a
humility of heart. We are to lead the flock, but never exploit it.
Shepherds are called to pour out their lives for the flock. In this
life there may be few rewards, but they are working for a crown
which will never tarnish. If you are a shepherd, you should work
for a shepherd's reward. And the essential qualification of a
shepherd is that he has a shepherd's heart.

Paul has the same sense of the high calling of ministry:

Keep watch over yourselves and all the flock of which the Holy
Spirit has made you overseers. Be shepherds of the church of
God, which he bought with his own blood.
(Acts 20:28)

The flock is so precious to Jesus that he shed his blood for it.
Christ died to redeem his people. It may be going too far to say
that God died, but we may affirm that the one who died was
God. What a privilege it is to serve this flock.

The Shepherd's model

As the good Shepherd, Jesus leaves us a model of what being a
shepherd should look like.

Strictly speaking, this model applies to those called to the
pastoral ministry. The elders or shepherds are to do this work.
However, every form of Christian leadership involves shepherding
of one kind or another. You may have to shepherd a youth group

or a home group. Your flock may be a cluster of kids or a gathering of elderly people. It could be an evangelistic course that you help run or maybe a family group. We are all called to encourage and pastor one another (Hebrews 10:24–25), making a deliberate and premeditated attempt to spur each other on in the faith.

Whatever the size and dynamics of the flock we lead, what is to mark us out as shepherds? John chapter 10 gives us a wonderful steer. Here Jesus identifies five characteristics of good shepherding:

The shepherd leads the flock (10:4). He is to give them a sense of direction and lead them forward to reach God-given goals. Most of us are suspicious of change, and yet a leader is supposed to be an agent of change. The sheep follow if they have come to recognize his voice and trust him. A good shepherd leads the flock – he does not drive it. The sheep watch and trust him, and readily follow him. In his book *Learning to Lead*, Chua Wee Hian describes a group of tourists visiting the Holy Land. Their guide described how the Eastern shepherd walks ahead of his flock and does not drive them from behind. While he was speaking, the group noticed a man in the distance harshly driving a flock of sheep. They pointed him out to the guide. He went across to the man and after a brief conversation announced, 'Ladies and gentlemen, he is not the shepherd. He is the butcher!'[1] Sadly, butchers, more interested in fleecing the flock than feeding it, have sometimes led God's sheep.

The shepherd defends the flock (10:5–10, 12). There are a whole host of bogus shepherds around. They come to kill and destroy. They exploit the vulnerable and confuse the gullible. They abuse trust and take advantage of the defenceless. The shepherd is to identify the danger and defend the flock.

Now false teachers are often very nice people. They may have charismatic and magnetic personalities. Their teaching seems incredibly plausible. Without becoming fanatical heresy hunters, shepherds identify the danger and defend the flock. Sometimes their main responsibility is to fight the wolves.

The shepherd is to help the sheep to experience fullness of life (10:10). Christ alone is the source of life for his people. The under-shepherd is to encourage healthy growth by pointing the sheep to him. This will come through the spiritual food of the Scriptures. Healthy sheep will have a good appetite. Much pastoral care comes through Word ministry too. So it may be formal and public: preaching and teaching, or it may be informal and private: one-to-one discipleship or counselling. But whatever it is, the Bible will be the most valuable and indispensable of the shepherd's tools.

The shepherd knows his sheep, and his sheep know him (10:14). In Jesus' day most sheep were kept for their wool rather than their meat. This meant that they would remain with the same shepherd for a long time. He would get to know them and recognize when they were in need. I guess that sheep differ from one another. I know that people do. The wise shepherd recognizes the needs of individual sheep, and he 'gathers the lambs in his arms and carries them close to his heart; he gently leads those that have young' (Isaiah 40:11). You cannot know the sheep unless you invest time in their lives. Paul puts it like this: 'We loved you so much, we were delighted to share with you not only the gospel of God but our lives as well' (1 Thessalonians 2:8).

The shepherd seeks after the sheep that are not currently part of the flock (10:16). In the context here, this probably refers to the gathering of Gentiles into God's flock. However, it is surely legitimate to apply this to the longing of the Shepherd to increase the size of his flock. He is to seek after those who have backslidden or who have never been part of the flock in the first place (Luke 15:1–7). The shepherd's heart is to be constantly seeking the blessing of those who are not yet safely within the fold. Pastoral care does not stop at the door of the church. We should always have an eye on those who are beyond its boundaries.

The Shepherd's sacrifice

However, we have not yet reached the heart of John 10. The supreme characteristic of the good Shepherd is that he lays down his life for God's flock (10:11, 15, 17). The cross of Jesus was not an afterthought; it was the whole purpose of his mission. The sheep were in danger, and he stood between them and deadly peril. The Shepherd dies – the sheep live.

His death was unique and unrepeatable. He died as an atoning sacrifice, taking the punishment that the flock deserved. He is the sacrificial Lamb who takes away the sins of the world (John 1:29).

And yet this is also a model for our ministry. Paul rejoices that he suffers for the sake of the church. Without suggesting that the perfect sacrifice of Christ is in some way insufficient, he fills up in his flesh what is lacking in it for the sake of the church (Colossians 1:24). If the church is to flourish, its shepherds must be willing to make sacrifices. They do not live for their own reputation or glory – they exist for the glory of God and for the good of the flock.

As Christians, we are followers of a crucified Saviour. Jesus called us to deny ourselves, take up our cross and follow him (Mark 8:34). In the first century only one kind of person carried a cross – a man on his way to his crucifixion. There was no hope of escape – he was a dead man walking. Throughout our world hundreds of thousands of Christians are suffering for their faith at this very moment. It is extremely likely that some will even die for their faith today. Even if we do not pay with our blood, we need to remind ourselves that Christian discipleship is not a pain-free zone.

This applies particularly to those who are called into leadership. Leaders are often the focal point of the world's opposition to the church (Acts 5:17–18, 40). We may not be called to die a martyr's death, but we are called to live a shepherd's life. As we have seen, this is a painful and demanding calling. We must be realistic. Paul speaks often of the cost of leadership (2 Corinthians 4:12; 6:3–10). He reminds Timothy, a fledgling leader, that he is engaged in a fierce and ferocious spiritual warfare (2 Timothy 2:3–4). He can honestly confess that he has strained every muscle to fulfil God's calling on his life: engaging in spiritual conflict; running a long and demanding race; standing firm and refusing to sacrifice his spiritual principles (2 Timothy 4:6–7). He has been sustained by the hope of the shepherd's reward (4:8).

Exercise: Focus on stress

Stress may be defined as a feeling of doubt about being able to cope, a perception that the resources available do not match the demands being made.

Work through this list of stress factors and try to identify the ones that you find particularly troubling:

- The workload is overwhelming. The job is never done, and the demands seem unreasonable.
- We have difficulty in balancing out the demands of family, career and church leadership. The pressures on our marriage and family can be crushing.
- We experience undeserved criticism and a chronic lack of appreciation. How do you lead people who don't want to be led? Churches can be places of unresolved conflict. Indeed, sometimes issues have not been addressed for

years. Nothing saps our energy more than the destructive skirmishes that exist in some churches.

- If we are in full-time ministry, there is sometimes a sense of insecurity and financial pressure which can dominate our thinking and sap our energy.
- Many leaders are perfectionists. This can be highly demanding and destructive to a healthy self-image.
- Satan hates us and will do anything he can to disrupt our ministry. This may include temptation and condemnation. He may launch an attack on our minds or our wills or our emotions. We are particularly vulnerable when we are tired. Sometimes our busyness eclipses this reality from our view. We rush around trying to put out fires, when our time would be much better spent praying or asking others for prayer.
- On top of all this, we face the sheer demands of a God-centred life. Sometimes the gap between our aspirations and the reality of our lives overwhelms us.

Count the cost

I have met a lot of disappointed leaders. I have talked with leaders who can scarcely conceal their bitterness. I have tried to help leaders who have become disillusioned with the church and yet continue because there is no alternative career path.

It is easy to be disenchanted with the job. The hours are long, the pay is low, the resources are sparse, and the successes are minimal. It all looked so attractive at the beginning, but our human energy has petered out. We continue doing what is expected, but have become cynical. It wasn't ever meant to be like this.

Many acknowledge that they are angry with the sheep. I was preaching in South Wales some years ago. My text was Isaiah 40:1–11, and I happened to mention that sheep must sometimes frustrate their shepherd. After the service a weather-beaten old boy came up and identified himself to me as a retired shepherd. In a beautiful lilting accent, he said, 'I can tell you, I have known hundreds of sheep and just as many people. Sheep can be difficult, but I have never met a sheep as difficult as a person!' People can indeed be frustrating and annoying. They can be awkward and ungrateful. They can take us for granted and misunderstand our best efforts, as we saw earlier.

Just a few will actually confess that they are angry with God. They feel that he has misled them or deserted them. Why didn't he make it clear that ministry was so costly?

If we have such feelings, we are not alone. At various times, Moses, Elijah and Jeremiah all felt abandoned by God (Numbers 11:15; 1 Kings 19:4; Jeremiah 20:18). They felt that their meagre resources were exhausted, and that in some way God had let them down.

We need to be gentle with wounded leaders, but the accusation that there were no warnings is ungrounded. The good Shepherd laid down his life for the sheep. We are called to follow in his footsteps. If there is one great leitmotif about leadership in the New Testament, it is that leaders must be prepared to suffer. We exist for the life of the flock, not vice versa.

We exist for the life of the flock, not vice versa.

It does not mean that we should be silly about things – our goal is neither to 'rust out' nor to burn out. God has given us our lives to spend for his glory. It is a mistake either to hoard it or waste it. Wisdom lies in spending it carefully.

Of course, there is more to it than counting the cost. We must also delight in Christ and keep our eyes on the reward that God has promised to faithful shepherds. This will be the subject of future chapters. However, this is a good focus for now.

If you want stay fresh in ministry, develop a good dose of realism. Yours is a high calling. God has called you to a pretty tough job. Forget the sanitized pictures in children's Bibles and stained-glass windows. Strap on your sandals, pick up your rod and staff, and get shepherding!

Questions

1. What is your flock?
2. Consider the list of stress factors above. What others might you add to the list?
3. Why are people difficult? How do you get to love the people whom you serve?
4. What is leadership costing you right now? How can you avoid becoming disillusioned?
5. How do we help all the members of the flock to recognize that they are called to a ministry of encouragement?

5. Fear God, not people

When he rang me, he was in a real state.

We had met at a conference and exchanged phone numbers. By this time, I had been in ministry for a decade. He was just beginning the adventure. His was a small church with a small congregation in a small village. He had to do some gardening work to supplement his meagre stipend. They survived because his wife also did some work from home while looking after their kids.

But money wasn't the problem. The problem was that the people he served were afraid of change.

I had come across this problem before. I had heard a radio interview with an old Wiltshire farmer who was just celebrating his hundredth birthday. He had lived in the house he was born in and worked on the farm that his grandad had farmed.

'You must have seen a lot of changes in your life,' the interviewer said.

'Yes,' the old boy replied, 'and I've been against every single one of them.'

He was probably an evangelical Christian!

My friend had run into this mentality, and it was really tough. When he accepted the call, he had said that he felt that the church would need to change if it was going to reach the village. They were so relieved at getting a pastor at all that they readily agreed. But now, eighteen months down the road, they were blocking him at every step.

'We want to grow – it's just that we don't want to change'

The final straw – what had prompted the impassioned phone call – had taken place that afternoon.

About six miles from the church there was a psychiatric unit for people with learning difficulties. One Sunday a resident had turned up. He had walked the six miles to find the church and, because he had little sense of time, had arrived a couple of hours early. He had sat at the back rolling cigarettes for his return journey. Apart from some issues of personal hygiene, he was no problem and posed no threat. He kept coming for a couple of months, and my friend fed him and told him about Christ. He would often take him back to the hospital after the evening service. The man seemed to be responding well, and my friend was encouraged.

And then he just stopped coming. My friend tried to follow him up, but the man said he didn't want to come any more, and he didn't give any reason.

However, it soon became clear that some of the members had felt unhappy about his presence in their church and, without saying anything, had gone out of their way to make him feel it. One of the ladies piously confessed that she had been praying that the man would not return. 'He does not fit our kind of church,' she said.

My friend was deeply disturbed and went to see the other church leader. He confessed his frustration. He had come here on the understanding that the church wanted to grow. The other man listened for a while and then said, 'You just don't understand the people in our church. Of course we want to grow – it's just that we don't want to change.'

Change is vital

What does it mean to be a leader? Whether it is leading a home group or a mission or a youth ministry or a soup-run, the answer is the same. A leader is an agent of change. Leadership means seeing how things are and how they could be. It is having the capacity to influence people so that they want to move towards God's purpose for their lives. Leaders are preoccupied with future possibilities, and they love to dream dreams about what could be.

True leadership should be vision-driven rather than maintenance-minded. Vision is seeing beyond what God has accomplished in the past to what God desires to accomplish in the future. Good leaders have a clear view of where God wants them to be and are passionately committed to getting there.

Now managing change can be a tricky thing. David Watson once advised caution: 'If you want to move the piano from one side of the platform to the other, do it six inches per week.' The idea is to make haste slowly. However, change we must.

Why are Christians sometimes afraid of change? There are many reasons for this. Very often it is a selfish desire to remain secure in my comfort zone. The world is a bewildering place; the only place where I feel safe is in church – please don't take my church away from me! And calling for change is sometimes seen as an implied criticism of the past. Are you saying that we have got it wrong all these years?

However, I believe that the most common motivation behind an antipathy to change is that a commitment to being conservative in theology sometimes leads to an equal commitment to being conservative in practice. God does not change. The ultimate purpose of God does not change. The gospel does not change, and our mission in the world does not change. Why should we change?

Let me confess – I am unashamedly conservative in my theological convictions. I am fully committed to the apostolic gospel, its defence and propagation. I do not believe that we have to tamper with the truth in order to make it more acceptable or relevant to modern people. We need to listen to their questions and speak their language while being loyal to the authentic gospel of Christ.

But that does not mean that nothing ever changes in the church. The Bible commands personal growth and dynamic transformation (Romans 12:1–2). Growth always implies change. Jesus expected his church to grow. When he addresses the seven churches in Asia Minor, he gently but firmly reminds them that they are not perfect and need to develop in particular areas (Revelation 2 – 3). All of the New Testament letters were written to elicit change of some sort.

The purpose of Christian ministry is to present everyone mature in Christ (Colossians 1:28–29). Maturity implies growth. We carefully monitor the growth of a baby because we want to make sure that she is developing in a healthy way. Growth demands change.

Change and vitality

What has this got to do with staying fresh in ministry?

That's a good question.

The friend I mentioned at the start of this chapter was very careful to guard his relationship with God. It is true that you can never fully know someone else's heart – it's hard enough to know your own. But from what I could see, he was a man who had the same struggles that we all have, and yet loved Christ, cared for his people and guarded his heart. What was wearing him down was the battle to bring about biblical change among a people who really didn't want it.

How do we stay fresh in these circumstances? How do we keep going when we feel thwarted at every step?

Some leaders don't have a problem here, because they are happy with maintenance rather than mission. When it comes to leading the charge against change, they are in the vanguard. If that is you, I would ask you to review the first part of the chapter. By the very nature of our calling, we are to be agents of change. That is not change for the sake of it, or irresponsible change or rash and reckless change. But if we are in any position of leadership, we must steel ourselves to the fact that growth is our goal and this is impossible without change.

What about those who are convinced and yet frustrated? You want the people to grow, but they are reluctant. You can see what your home group or youth group or evangelistic meeting could become, but feel frustrated. Retreating into the intimacy of our relationship with God is not enough. Don't give up on the possibility of transformation.

By the very nature of our calling, we are to be agents of change.

Let me make a few suggestions.

Be strong and show yourself a man (or woman)

King David well knew the pressures and trials of leadership. He knew the importance of integrity and the need for boldness in leading the people of God. When he came to the end of his life, he summoned Solomon, his successor, and gave him this charge:

> 'I am about to go the way of all the earth,' he said. 'So be strong, act like a man, and observe what the LORD your God requires: walk in obedience to him, and keep his decrees and commands, his laws and regulations, as written in the Law of Moses. Do this so that you may prosper in all you do and wherever you go and that the LORD may keep his promise to me: "If your descendants watch how they live, and if they walk faithfully before me with all their heart and soul, you will never fail to have a successor on the throne of Israel."'
> (1 Kings 2:2–4)

David was driven by the conviction that God had set clear guidelines on how his people were to be ruled. Leaders need to guard their relationship with God and allow his will to shape their direction. If they are to do this, they will need courage. Hence the command to display the bold characteristics sometimes associated with mature masculinity. Of course, some of the bravest people in the Bible were women! But the point remains the same: any form of leadership demands courage.

Christian leaders must be driven by clear theological convictions. Why would you want to be a leader if you did not have strong convictions? While remaining humble, and distrustful of our own abilities, we need to know what we believe and why we believe it.

Instituting change demands courage. Most of us want a peaceful life, but when we champion change, we find that we meet resistance and at times downright hostility. Sometimes it comes from outsiders, sometimes from the people we lead. And sometimes it comes from our fellow leaders.

The Baptist pastor C. H. Spurgeon once warned, 'If you resist Satan he will fly from you. If you resist one of your deacons he will fly at you!' It is easy to lose our nerve in such circumstances and to back away from our convictions.

But this is always a dangerous thing to do. If we abandon our convictions because we are afraid of how people will react, then we have also abandoned our mandate to lead. The 'fear of man' has become a 'snare' (Proverbs 29:25). Like the jaws of a trap closing on the leg of a struggling animal, fear has caught hold of us. It will not let us go, limiting our freedom and capacity for movement. We are tethered to the spot and cannot take the church forward into all that God might have for it.

Be strong and very courageous

Courage is vital for leadership. Paul reminds Timothy, his young protégé,

> For this reason I remind you to fan into flame the gift of
> God, which is in you through the laying on of my hands.
> For the Spirit God gave us does not make us timid, but
> gives us power, love and self-discipline. So do not be
> ashamed of the testimony about our Lord or of me his
> prisoner. Rather, join with me in suffering for the gospel,
> by the power of God.
> (2 Timothy 1:6–8)

There is a cost to leadership – Paul is in prison as he writes. Timothy may be tempted to abandon his post and to back away, forgetting to fan the flame of his service. In response to this, Paul reminds him that timidity is not a mark of the presence of the Holy Spirit. The Spirit gives us power and love and self-discipline. This is a power that fosters confidence in God and results in renewed courage. It is a love that makes us bold to take risks because we want the people we serve to grow and flourish in the things of God. It is a self-control that helps us to subdue the fears and anxieties which sometimes arise in our hearts.

Courage is not something that we muster up. It is something that God willingly gives us through the gracious agency of his life-giving Spirit. That is why Jesus told the disciples to wait for the coming of the Spirit on the day of Pentecost. He would lead them into the truth, teach them what to say and give them boldness to say it. That is why the early Christians prayed for boldness and then, filled with the Spirit, proclaimed the word of God boldly (Acts 4:31). That is why the first 'deacons' of the church, set aside for practical ministry in Acts 6, were to be Spirit-filled men.

It may sound slightly simplistic, but 'courage is fear that has said its prayers'.[1] And when we pray, what do we pray for? That God would give us the gift of the Spirit of boldness so that we can lead his people without fear or favour.

Remember who you serve

In Acts 3 – 4 the young church faces persecution for the first time. Peter has preached boldly about Christ:

> Salvation is found in no one else, for there is no other name under heaven given to mankind by which we must be saved.
> (Acts 4:12)

The religious authorities feel threatened and warn Peter and John not to preach or teach in the name of Jesus (4:18). Their response is stunning:

> But Peter and John replied, 'Which is right in God's eyes: to listen to you, or to him? You be the judges! As for us, we cannot help speaking about what we have seen and heard.'
> (Acts 4:19–20)

It's quite simple – in a clear choice between obeying Jesus or obeying people, they had to go with Jesus every time. They had no alternative – and neither do we today. In the Acts 3 – 4 situation the hostility came from outside. And in some ways that is easier to handle. I expect opposition from the world. It's when resistance to biblical change comes from fellow Christians that the problem becomes more acute.

But the solution is the same. Just like the apostles, we need to remember whom we serve. We live before the face of God. We are captivated by his cause and are ultimately answerable to him alone.

I want the people that I serve to like me. I would have a very quirky personality if I didn't. I want to do the best I can to secure their love and to build warm and lasting relationships with them. I want to avoid conflict if at all possible. Sometimes I have to sacrifice my own convictions about secondary and unimportant things for the sake of harmony. Often the things we think are fundamental non-negotiables turn out to be matters of taste and personal preference.

But although all these things may be true, there comes a point when, if I am to lead with honesty and integrity, I will need to have the courage to stand by my convictions. We serve God, not people. We must never compromise our consciences – the moment we do, we will be in trouble.

Paul often faced this choice, but never more so than in his battles with the church at Corinth. He often had to display great wisdom and courage in his dealings with this difficult church. What gave him the boldness to challenge their sin and demand reformation? He knew that he was a servant of Christ, answerable to him. Listen to his words:

> For we must all appear before the judgment seat of Christ,
> so that each of us may receive what is due us for the things
> done while in the body, whether good or bad. Since, then,
> we know what it is to fear the Lord, we try to persuade others.
> What we are is plain to God, and I hope it is also plain to your
> conscience.
> (2 Corinthians 5:10–11)

Experience the fear that drives out fear

Paul talks about the 'fear of the Lord'. Here is the paradoxical message of the Bible: it is only fear that drives out fear.

Some people are pretty intimidating. The way to deal with this problem is to fear God more than people. After all, God is more powerful and potentially more frightening than the most frightening bunch of people that we have ever met.

At the heart of biblical religion is the fear of the Lord, that sense of awe, respect and wonder which we feel when we meditate on the character and activities of the living God. It involves a reverence for his majesty and a submission to his authority. It goes hand in hand with love and is never set over against it. Thus we can read the words of Moses:

> And now, Israel, what does the LORD your God ask of you but to fear the LORD your God, to walk in obedience to him, to love him, to serve the LORD your God with all your heart and with all your soul, and to observe the LORD's commands and decrees that I am giving you today for your own good?
> (Deuteronomy 10:12–13)

There is also no conflict between fear and joy. In our worship we are to 'Serve the LORD with fear and celebrate his rule with trembling' (Psalm 2:11).

When we think how great God is, this seems pretty obvious. Staying fresh in ministry means a daily encounter with the God who is awesomely holy. This is the place where wisdom starts and courage grows (Proverbs 1:7).

God called Isaiah to deliver a painful and demanding message to a group of people who would not listen – indeed, God seems to guarantee almost complete failure (Isaiah 6:9–12) with just a brief glimpse of hope (6:13). How could Isaiah persevere in the face of either stony indifference or outright opposition? The answer is that God gave him a vision of his transcendent glory and magnificence (Isaiah 6:1–4). The revelation of God's awesome majesty and absolute purity led to a humble confession of sin (6:5), a gracious act of cleansing (6:6–7) and a compelling call to service. I am sure that Isaiah never forgot this encounter. Throughout his ministry he refers to God as the 'Holy One of Israel'.

Commenting on this passage, John Piper says,

> People are starving for the greatness of God. But most of them would not give this diagnosis of their troubled lives. The majesty of God is the unknown cure. There are far more popular prescriptions on the market, but the benefits of any

other remedy are brief and shallow. Preaching that does not have the aroma of God's greatness may entertain for a season, but it will not touch the hidden cry of the soul: Show me your glory![2]

Be faithful servants

Piper is right. If we are to be effective Christians, our lives must be shaped by the contemplation of the glory of God and the holy joy and loving fear that this will inspire. This is doubly so if we are to engage in Christian leadership.

So, as we regularly meet this God in his Word, we will be able to affirm and ask with the psalmist,

> In God I trust and am not afraid.
>   What can mere mortals do to me?
> (Psalm 56:4)

We will heed the warnings of Jesus:

> I tell you, my friends, do not be afraid of those who kill the body and after that can do no more. But I will show you whom you should fear: fear him who, after your body has been killed, has authority to throw you into hell. Yes, I tell you, fear him.
> (Luke 12:4–5)

And we will listen to the instructions of Peter:

> But even if you should suffer for what is right, you are blessed. 'Do not fear their threats; do not be frightened.' But in your hearts revere Christ as Lord. Always be prepared to give an answer to everyone who asks you to give the reason for the hope that you have.
> (1 Peter 3:14–15)

What constitutes a successful ministry? What does it look like? What is its shape? We might come up with all sorts of ways of measuring success, but in the end all that matters is pleasing God. And what does he look for? The answer is faithfulness (1 Corinthians 4:1–2).

This may sound a little cosy and twee, a kind of excuse for inactivity, but nothing could be further from the truth. Real faithfulness is courageous and adventurous. It takes risks of faith because it trusts God to multiply blessings in response to trusting him and stepping out in faith (Matthew 14:22–36). This is the kind of courage that causes Abram to leave everything he knows and to follow wherever God leads him (Genesis 12:1–3). It is the boldness which enables Stephen to preach to a hostile crowd and pray for their forgiveness as rocks rain down on his head (Acts 7:1 – 8:1). And it is the sheer bravery which took Jesus to the cross in obedience to his Father's will (Mark 14:32–42; John 12:27–28).

Leadership demands courage, and courage grows out of the knowledge of God: '. . . the people that do know their God shall be strong, and do exploits' (Daniel 11:32 KJV).

Questions

1. How do we distinguish between non-negotiable matters of integrity and secondary issues of personal preference or taste?
2. Why do people resist change? How do we love the people who oppose it?
3. Where do we find the courage we need to serve God faithfully in spite of opposition and conflict?
4. Using a concordance, put together a list of verses about the fear of the Lord. What are the benefits and blessings of fearing God?

6. Take time to be holy

My wife and I began married life at a church which had no full-time pastor. This meant that we had a number of visiting itinerant preachers on Sundays.

There was one old boy whom we both loved. He was a Wiltshire farmer who wrote his sermons while sitting on his tractor. He was clearly no great scholar, but he certainly had a way with words and a fine turn of phrase. He was self-effacing and would sometimes defend his lack of book learning with the quaint old saying: 'Wiltshire born and Wiltshire bred, strong in the arm and thick in the head'.

Coming from Birmingham, we had never heard anything quite like this before. However, we soon came to enjoy his visits, because his preaching was very powerful – he knew God and he knew his Bible.

'This body of death'

He also knew the human heart. When he preached, he seemed to uncover the deep springs of the heart and lay them bare.

One Sunday he preached from Romans 7. Here Paul is describing the battle that rages in his soul. There is a whole range of possible interpretations, but I am personally persuaded that the chapter describes the conflict within the heart of every Christian. A struggle exists between our old sinful nature and our new spiritual one. Since conversion, we are like a walking civil war.

That morning the preacher shared my interpretation. He came towards the end of the passage:

> So I find this law at work: although I want to do good, evil is right there with me. For in my inner being I delight in God's law; but I see another law at work in me, waging war against the law of my mind and making me a prisoner of the law of sin at work within me. What a wretched man I am! Who will rescue me from this body that is subject to death? Thanks be to God, who delivers me through Jesus Christ our Lord!
> (Romans 7:21–25)

Our farming friend described his own internal struggles and the daily battle he felt raging in his soul. Then he leaned across the pulpit, as preachers do when they want to drive a point home, and said something like this:

> Look at that cry – 'Who will rescue me from this body of death?' Those old Romans were a cruel bunch. They knew how to torture a man. Sometimes they would take a rotting corpse and chain it to the body of a living man they wanted to punish. He would be pressed up against the corpse – leg to leg, chest to chest, face to face and mouth to mouth. Can you imagine? Breathing in death, desperate to get rid of the dead flesh, but unable to break free. That's how Paul felt. And that's how I feel. I hate sin, but I cannot get rid of it. Neither can you.

I don't know if he was correct about the Romans – I have never been able to verify his statement – but what an evocative image!

He was certainly correct in his diagnosis of my heart. Since I first became a Christian, I have longed to live for Christ and to please him. I have longed to be holy. And at the same time I have felt the downward pull of the old nature. It may be dead, but it won't lie down.

And I'm not alone. This is the battle we all face as Christian disciples and as Christian leaders.

Guard your heart

Our battle with sin is not 'out there'. It is inward and intensely personal. The battleground is the Christian's heart.

But what do we mean by the heart? We tend to think of the heart as the centre of our emotions – a combination of feelings and affections. It is often contrasted with the mind or reason. But the Bible uses the word 'heart' in a different way. It is something deeper and more comprehensive than both reason and emotion. The heart is the deep inner driving force at the centre of all that we are. It is what steers us and shapes us and determines our decisions. It is your authentic self – the core of your being. It is where all our dreams, our desires and our passions live.

King Solomon warns us,

Above all else, guard your heart,
    for everything you do flows from it.
(Proverbs 4:23)

The heart is like a spring from which waters flow. If your heart is pure, your thoughts and desires and words and actions will be pure. If the spring is poisoned, then all that flows from it will become toxic. If our heart is unhealthy, it has an impact on everything else – our marriage and family, our relationships and our leadership.

No wonder Jesus speaks of the heart as he does.

What comes out of a person is what defiles them. For it is
from within, out of a person's heart, that evil thoughts come –
sexual immorality, theft, murder, adultery, greed, malice, deceit,
lewdness, envy, slander, arrogance and folly. All these evils come
from inside and defile a person.
(Mark 7:20–23)

Fight the greatest leadership battle of all

And here is my greatest problem as a Christian leader: my heart
is a battleground.

When I became a Christian, God gave me a new heart. At the
deepest core of my being, I delight in God and want to love him
and serve him. But at the very same time I feel another tug, away
from God and towards my own self-centred desires and passions.
In spite of my best efforts, it is an ever-present reality. It feels just
like an unwelcome corpse chained to me. I can smell its decay
and taste its rot. It is vile and rancid and corrupt. The longer I
live as a Christian, the more I hate the battle that no-one else
sees. It is the battle for holiness, the crusade against lust and
greed and sloth and envy and anger and bitterness and pride.

But thank God for his grace! Because of it I am slowly making
progress. Yet sometimes the progress seems so slow and the
regress so easy. Sometimes the sins that I thought I had conquered
a long time ago return with a fresh vigour and a new lease of
malignant life. Sometimes I feel a total hypocrite as I step into
the pulpit and seek to point others along a road which I am so
inadequately following myself. I want to do good, but evil seems
closer and much easier. In my heart of hearts I delight in Christ
– his Word, his will, his way. But there is an alien force inside me,
fighting a vicious guerrilla war: 'What a wretched man I am!
Who will rescue me from this body that is subject to death?'

So the greatest battle in Christian leadership is the battle for holiness.

Be holy because I am holy

God saved us in order to make us holy.

Holiness is not an optional extra reserved for a special class of Christian converts – it is the reason why God redeemed us in the first place. God rescued Israel from slavery, oppression and certain death in Egypt. When they eventually arrived at Mount Sinai, God reminded them that they belonged to him and that he had saved them so that they would become a kingdom of priests and a holy nation (Exodus 19:3–6). Israel were to be distinct from every other nation, 'commissioned with sharing and displaying the divine nature and the likeness of God their Saviour'.[1]

And this same imperative is laid upon us (1 Peter 2:5). God the Father chose us in Christ before the foundation of the world, so that we should be holy (Ephesians 1:4). God the Son shed his blood to purify a people so that they would be a holy and pure bride (Ephesians 5:25–27). The agenda of God the Holy Spirit is to transform us so that we become holy (2 Corinthians 3:17–18). The deliberate and determined design of the triune God is to bring a holy people into existence.

The greatest thing God does today is to take a sinful man or woman out of a sinful world, make them holy, put them back in a sinful world and keep them holy.

In his monumental book *Holiness*, Bishop J. C. Ryle expressed it like this:

> We must be holy, because this is the one grand end and purpose for which Christ came into the world . . . Jesus is a complete Saviour. He does not merely take away the guilt of the believer's sin, he does more – he breaks its power (1 Peter 1:2; Romans 8:29; 2 Timothy 1:9; Hebrews 12:10).[2]

Cultivate the inner man

We minister and serve out of the context of our character. Robert Murray M'Cheyne (1813–43) was a pastor in Dundee who died of typhus at the age of twenty-nine in 1843 and was buried in his own churchyard. Two years after his death, his friend Andrew Bonar published *Memoir and Remains of Robert Murray M'Cheyne*.[3] It is one of the most moving and powerful accounts of the inner life and struggles of a man of God, recording the longing for holiness and the passion for purity that are essential for Christian leadership.

Why is holiness so important? Listen to the words of M'Cheyne:

> Do not forget the culture of the inner man – I mean of the heart. How diligently the cavalry officer keeps his sabre clean and sharp; every stain he rubs off with the greatest care. Remember you are God's sword, his instrument – I trust, a chosen vessel unto Him to bear His name. In great measure, according to the purity and perfection of the instrument, will be the success. It is not great talents God blesses so much as likeness to Jesus. A holy minister is an awful weapon in the hand of God.[4]

Conviction is vital and competence is essential for effective Christian leadership. But the primary demand is for holiness of character.

Exercise: Quotations from Robert Murray M'Cheyne

Take some time to meditate on these quotations from *Memoir and Remains of Robert Murray M'Cheyne*. What do they teach you about leadership?

'A man is what he is on his knees before God, and nothing more.'

'The Christian is a person who makes it easy for others to believe in God.'

'Study universal holiness of life. Your whole usefulness depends on this, for your sermons last but an hour or two; your life preaches all the week. If Satan can only make a covetous minister a lover of praise, of pleasure, of good eating, he has ruined your ministry. Give yourself to prayer, and get your texts, your thoughts, your words from God. Luther spent his best three hours in prayer.'

'Live near to God, and all things will appear little to you in comparison with eternal realities.'

'A great part of my time is spent in getting my heart in tune for prayer. It is the link that connects earth with heaven.'

'Lord, make me as holy as a pardoned sinner can be.'

'Oh how sweet to work for God all day, and then lie down at night beneath His smile.'

'The greatest need of my people is my personal holiness.'

'Unfathomable oceans of grace are in Christ for you. Dive and dive again, you will never come to the bottom of these depths. How many millions of dazzling pearls and gems are at this moment hid in the deep recesses of the ocean caves.'

Focus on holiness

The word 'holy' occurs more than 600 times in the Bible. Its first use is in Genesis 2:3 where God is blessing the seventh day and setting it aside to be different from other days – a day of blessing for his people. As we read on in the Bible, we find holy places and holy people and holy objects. In each case they are set aside from ordinary use for God's purposes.

Holy things are separate and distinct. The supreme example of holiness is God himself. He is marked out by awesome majesty and absolute purity. This is why Moses sings,

> Who among the gods
>   is like you, LORD?
> Who is like you –
>   majestic in holiness,
> awesome in glory,
>   working wonders?
> (Exodus 15:11)

We reflect God's holiness in an inadequate way. But because he is the image of the invisible God and the exact representation of his being (Colossians 1:15; Hebrews 1:3), Jesus displays God's holiness perfectly. In the life of Christ we see what a life of holiness should look like. And God's ultimate purpose is to make us like Jesus:

> For those God foreknew he also predestined to be conformed to the image of his Son, that he might be the firstborn among many brothers and sisters.
> (Romans 8:29)

We belong to God's family – Jesus is the first among many brothers and sisters. Sanctification, the process of making us holy, is the slow but sure transformation of adopted children so that they bear the family likeness. It is the lifelong process of making us like Jesus. It is not just obedience to a set of external rules, although the biblical commands do express God's will and give us a pattern to follow. It is the inner transformation of the heart so that we love what Jesus loves and hate what Jesus hates and begin to resemble him in all his loveliness.

And we will never be faithful and effective Christian leaders unless we are living Christlike lives.

So what do we need to do? That will be the subject of our next chapter.

But before we move on, try the exercise below:

Exercise: Why should we be holy?

In his great book on holiness, J. C. Ryle outlines eight reasons why holiness is important:

- We must be holy because the voice of God in Scripture plainly commands it (Matthew 5:20, 48; 1 Thessalonians 4:3; 1 Peter 1:15).
- We must be holy because it is the one grand end and purpose for which Christ came into the world (Romans 8:29; 2 Corinthians 5:15; Ephesians 5:25–26; Titus 2:14; Hebrews 12:10).
- We must be holy because it is the only sound evidence that we have a saving faith in Jesus Christ (James 2:17).
- We must be holy because it is the only proof that we love the Lord Jesus Christ in sincerity (John 14:15, 21, 23; 15:14).
- We must be holy because it is the only sound evidence that we are children of God (John 8:39, 42; Romans 8:14).
- We must be holy because it is the most likely way that we can do good to others in this world (1 Peter 3:1).
- We must be holy because our present comforts depend much upon it (Acts 5:41; 1 John 2:3; 3:19).
- We must be holy because without holiness on earth we will never be prepared to enjoy heaven (Revelation 21:27).

1. Look up the Bible references and consider the arguments that Ryle uses. What conclusions do you draw?

---

2. Why is holiness essential to Christian leadership?
3. What are the dangers for the church when leaders are not passionately committed to the pursuit of holiness?

7. Take more time to be holy

Let me introduce you to Andy.

When he first came to church, Andy struggled with bad language. He worked on the factory floor and punctuated his conversation with expletives. After one of our church services he told me that he wanted to become a Christian, but knew that he had to clean up his mouth before God would accept him. I explained that this was the wrong way round: 'You don't need to clean up your life so that Jesus will accept you. If you wait until you are better, you will never come. You want to change? Come as you are, and Jesus will clean up your mouth.'

So he came to Christ, and Christ changed his speech almost overnight.

After he had been a Christian for almost six months, Andy came to see me. He was distraught. He had lost his temper at work and given someone a mouthful. Immediately he was overwhelmed with guilt and a feeling of despair.

'It's no good,' he told me. 'I'm not a real Christian. When I first came to Jesus, I was so full of joy. But now it is such a slog. I love him more than anything, but there is something inside me that keeps heading off in the wrong direction. It's like a battle inside. I want to win, but sometimes I fail. I can't be a real Christian, can I?'

He must have wondered why I was smiling while he told me his story: 'Welcome to the club, Andy. What you tell me pretty well assures me that you must be a Christian. Only real Christians feel that conflict.'

The desires of the flesh

I knew where Andy was coming from because I had been there myself. So have you. We can have the most wonderful prayer time or listen to the most powerful sermon or attend the most affirming home group, and then suddenly unwelcome and un-helpful thoughts fill our mind. Sometimes we resist them and they go away. On other occasions we indulge them. The thought becomes a plan and the plan becomes an action, and before we know it, we have fallen into a pattern of sinful behaviour. We need to repent and return to God and put it right before we can go on. No wonder Jesus taught us to pray for forgiveness every single day (Matthew 6:12; 1 John 1:8 – 2:2).

Paul also refers to this conflict in Galatians 5: 'For the flesh desires what is contrary to the Spirit, and the Spirit what is contrary to the flesh. They are in conflict with each other, so that you are not to do whatever you want' (5:17).

There is an alien in the camp.

Christians are walking civil wars. Within the same person the flesh and the Spirit coexist. We have become a new creation in Christ, and therefore God has sent his Spirit to dwell in us. The Spirit animates and gives life to our new nature. We have new passions and desires. We want to please Christ and live for his glory. But against this, we have an old sinful nature – 'the flesh' – that old body of death which pulls us down and causes us to do the very opposite from what we really want to do.

When Paul talks about the 'desires' of the flesh and the Spirit, he uses a word that means 'to yearn' or 'to crave'. The flesh and the Spirit yearn for diametrically opposite things. The biggest battle we face is not 'out there' – it is within us. There is an alien in the camp.

And this battle is lifelong. We can never relax. There is no discharge in this war.

Walk in the Spirit

So what does my old fallen nature – that alien in the camp – yearn for? Paul gives us a long and ugly list (Galatians 5:19–21). This is what life without grace looks like. Fifteen separate characteristics find their way onto Paul's list. They include sexual sins (sexual immorality, impurity and debauchery), religious sins (idolatry and witchcraft), social sins (hatred, discord, jealousy, fits of rage, selfish ambition, dissensions, factions and envy) and sins of excess (drunkenness, orgies). And the catalogue is not exhaustive, since Paul ends with: 'and the like' (5:21).

Paul concludes with a fearful warning. Because we have an old and fallen nature, we may easily fall in any of these areas. However, anyone who lives a careless lifestyle, unconcerned about these sins and happily indulging in them, proves that they do not have a new nature. Such people will not inherit the kingdom of God.

But that's not the whole picture. Around the warning in Galatians 5:17 Paul wraps a command to walk in the Spirit (5:16) and a promise to those who are led by the Spirit (5:18). The Holy Spirit is an active presence – the life of God in the soul of man. He cultivates and strengthens the new nature that he gave us when we were born again. He is at work in our hearts giving us new desires and new affections and new longings. This means that, for the Christian, the new nature is the dominant power at work within.

And what does the new nature yearn for?

Paul uses the image of the 'fruit of the Spirit' (Galatians 5:22–23). Fruit describes what we really are. This is a description of the normal, balanced Christian life, a life directed by the Spirit. There is a deep yearning to be like Jesus. It covers our relationship with God (love, joy, peace), our relationship with others (forbearance, kindness, goodness) and three inner qualities or virtues (faithfulness, gentleness and self-control).

The work of the Spirit

God makes us holy through the influence of the Holy Spirit mediated through the Word of God. The Spirit cultivates and fortifies the new nature. He gives us holy desires in the first place and helps us to see them come to fruition. I knew that Andy was a Christian, because only a Christian hates sin and longs for release from its power as he did. The Spirit sets us apart to belong to Christ and works in us so that we can obey God's commands (1 Peter 1:2). He strengthens us in our inner being (Ephesians 3:16). He shines the light of truth into the dark recesses of our hearts and convicts us of our sin (John 16:7–11). He reveals Christ to us and gives us the longing to be like him (2 Corinthians 3:18).

There would be no holiness without the work of the Spirit. Without his help, our efforts amount to an unsuccessful and soul-sapping form of self-righteous moralism.

The Holy Spirit – and us

Yes, we need the supernatural aid and support of God's Spirit if we are to grow in holiness. However, we must not imagine for one moment that the Spirit blesses passivism or spiritual inertia.

The Bible is full of commands to work hard and to cooperate with the Spirit in this process of sanctification.

Consider the following commands:

- We are to offer our bodies as living sacrifices to God (Romans 12:1–2).
- We must hate what is evil and cling to what is good (Romans 12:9).
- We must not sow to please the sinful nature, but instead sow to please the Spirit. We must not become weary in well doing (Galatians 6:7–9).
- We must deliberately seek to be imitators of God and live a life of love (Ephesians 5:1–2).
- We must be strong in the Lord, put on the whole armour of God and stand firm (Ephesians 6:10–13).
- We must deliberately adopt the mind of Christ, thinking and behaving like him (Philippians 2:5).
- We must work out our salvation with fear and trembling (Philippians 2:12–13).
- We must set our minds on things above (Colossians 3:1–2).
- We must put the old nature to death (Colossians 3:5).
- We must clothe ourselves with compassion and love (Colossians 3:12–14).
- We must live to please God (1 Thessalonians 4:1–3).
- We must flee from evil and pursue righteousness (1 Timothy 6:11).
- We must make our calling and election sure (2 Peter 1:10).

I could highlight many more biblical imperatives. In each case there are clear and specific commands. Some Christians are afraid of emphasizing this. It's as if 'duty' is a dirty word. But it isn't. This is not a new form of legalism – it is the basic demand of a God-centred life.

And as we saw in the previous chapter, any leader who wants to be effective and maintain his or her vitality and spiritual usefulness must live a God-centred life.

But how?

Learn from the white dog and the black dog

I once heard a story about an old Inuit fisherman who visited town every Saturday afternoon. He owned two dogs – one was white and the other was black. On each occasion the other fishermen would gather in the town square and the dogs would fight. The men would take bets on the outcome, but somehow the owner of the battling canines would always know the eventual result. One day he was persuaded to reveal his secret.

'It's very simple,' he said. 'One week I feed the white dog and starve the black one. The white dog is strong and wins the fight. The next week I do it the other way round.'

Not a story for dog lovers, I'm afraid! However, it helps us to picture the way in which the process of sanctification works.

If you look carefully at the series of commands in the previous section, you will see that some are negatives (prohibitions) and others are positives (imperatives). There are things we must avoid and things we must cultivate.

Consider Paul's words to Timothy, a young Christian leader: 'But you, man of God, flee from all this, and pursue righteousness, godliness, faith, love, endurance and gentleness' (1 Timothy 6:11).

Like a runner in a race, there are things to run from and things to run after.

Coming back to our Inuit friend, you will remember that his secret was to feed one dog and starve the other. If we have an old and a new nature, then the secret of sanctification is to starve the old nature and its desires and to feed the new one and its longings.

Mortification

The old word 'mortification' sounds rather medieval. It conjures up musty cells in which half-starved monks are trying to beat their bodies into submission.

But this is not what the Bible means when it uses this word. The Bible commands,

> Put to death, therefore, whatever belongs to your earthly nature: sexual immorality, impurity, lust, evil desires and greed, which is idolatry. Because of these, the wrath of God is coming. You used to walk in these ways, in the life you once lived. But now you must also rid yourselves of all such things as these: anger, rage, malice, slander, and filthy language from your lips.
> (Colossians 3:5–8)

When it comes to the old nature, we are not to give it an inch. We are to strangle and stifle and stab it. We must shoot it, starve it and slaughter it. We have to hassle and hang it, choke and kill it, knife it and nuke it!

You get the picture. We must not allow it to control us. If your eye causes you to sin, pluck it out. We must not flirt with sin, but flee from it.

A few years ago I was speaking at a conference in Buckie, on the beautiful Moray Firth coast of Scotland. During a free afternoon a local fisherman took me out in his boat to catch some crabs. He had been a crab fisherman all his life, and I was impressed by the way he hauled the crustaceans on board. I noticed, however, that he was very careful about the way in which he picked them up and placed them in the basket. When I commented on this, he smiled and informed me, 'Of course I'm careful. They are fierce wee creatures. They are fresh from the sea and angry with it. I've seen a crab catch hold of a man's hand and it won't let it go. I've seen it break a man's finger rather than let go.'

'So what do you do if a crab does get hold of you?' I asked. At that moment it seemed a fairly relevant question!

'The only way to break its grip is to smash the crab against the side of the boat. If you don't kill it, it will hurt you.'

That sounds pretty radical, but it's exactly what Paul is saying in Colossians 3:5–7. If we don't break sin, it will break us. If we fail to take it seriously, it will ruin our lives and mar our ministry. Paul was conscious of the danger of allowing sin to disqualify him from service: 'No, I strike a blow to my body and make it my slave so that after I have preached to others, I myself will not be disqualified for the prize' (1 Corinthians 9:27).

I don't think he is talking about some weird form of self-flagellation. It is a reference to the self-discipline that is demanded of successful athletes. The Olympic medallist does not allow his body to control him. In matters of diet and exercise and the sacrifice of everyday pleasures, he keeps his body in check. Likewise, Christian leaders are called to a life of everyday sacrifice.

Avoid the edge

What does this mean in practice? We need to know ourselves and our own predispositions towards sin, and then refuse to indulge them. If the films we watch or the websites we visit or the friendships we cultivate or the hobbies we pursue feed the old nature with its sinful desires, then we must cut them out of our lives. This is certainly not a call for unhealthy abstention or morbid asceticism. Rather, it is a call to identify the things that have an unhealthy influence on our Christian lives and to refuse to allow them to control us.

When my kids were small, we used to let them play on a slide in a local recreation area. It was very steep and highly polished, and they called it the 'death slide'. One son would launch himself into the air without a care for the consequences. The other would sit on the rim of the slide with his legs dangling over the edge looking down into the jaws of polished metal. He could not be moved by any of our persuasive comments. No way was he going down there! Except that sometimes he would get just too close to the edge, and gravity would take over. Against his will, the slide would claim another victim!

There is a gravity about sin. We feel its constant pull and terrible potency. What is the answer? We will never defeat it in this life, but we can all stay away from the edge.

Exercise: The all-pervasive plague of pornography

One of the greatest challenges to maintaining a holy heart today is the all-pervasive plague of pornography. The increase of this problem is compounded by its accessibility, affordability and anonymity. I know from speaking to Christian leaders from a variety of backgrounds that this is a struggle for many of them. It is too complex a problem to deal with in this book. If you want to pursue it further, I would recommend *Captured by a Better Vision* by Tim Chester (IVP, 2010).

If this is your problem, then work through the following:

- Recognize that visiting pornographic sites is sinful – there should be no hint of sexual immorality in our lives (Matthew 5:27–30; Ephesians 5:3–5).
- Hate porn for what it is – not just for the shame it brings.
- Remember that God sees every website we visit.
- Acknowledge and accept that porn is not a 'victimless crime'. It has many unhealthy consequences:

  - It exploits and abuses people;
  - It undermines barriers and leads to other sins;
  - It erodes character and enslaves us;
  - It is a sin against your partner, and it ruins relationships.

- Recognize the danger signs. It is often triggered by boredom, loneliness, overwork, stress and self-pity. For Christian leaders, it is often a cheap and easy form of escape from a stressful situation. It is also an easy form of sexual release when the emotional demands of caring

for people mean that the leader has little emotional capital
to invest in his marriage.
- Avoid temptation – stay away from the edge and be radical
  about sin (Matthew 5:27–30).
- Develop a clear strategy:

  - Use Net Nanny or Covenant Eyes or an internet filter;
  - Keep your computer in a public place;
  - Go to bed at the same time as everyone else in your home;
  - Recognize the danger signs.

- However, know that God forgives sin. Failure isn't final
  (Psalm 32:1–2; 1 John 1:9 – 2:2).

Feed the new nature

There is more to spiritual growth than avoiding sin, although this
is sometimes the way in which Christian discipleship is carica-
tured. It is portrayed as a series of negatives: Christians are known
for what they don't do rather than for what they actually do. 'I
don't smoke and I don't chew and I don't go with girls who do.'[1]

As we have seen, the negative is important: we must make a
deliberate effort to conquer the sins that cling so closely to us.
However, real Christian holiness is amazingly life-affirming. It is
a manifestation of the character and beauty of Christ. Although
he was pure and sinless, sinners fled to him because of the personal
magnetism of a life full of grace and truth. And we are meant to
be like Jesus, to make him visible, intelligible and desirable.

This means that we need to feed the spiritual nature. But how?
Spiritual life needs spiritual food. We need a balanced diet which
will include several ingredients. Here are three:

- *We need a daily intake of biblical truth.* As the children's
  chorus used to remind us, 'Read your Bible, pray every
  day, if you want to grow . . .' We have to read and pray in

order to meet with God and see Jesus in his Word. It is as we gaze at Christ, illuminated by the Holy Spirit, that we will begin to become like him (2 Corinthians 3:17–18). We need to hide God's Word in our hearts and to meditate on Scripture so that it shapes our thinking and behaviour.

- *We need a healthy and health-giving life of prayer.* The Bible commands us to pray without ceasing (1 Thessalonians 5:17). In Psalm 27:4 David describes prayer as dwelling in God's presence, gazing on God's beauty and seeking God's help. It is not just following a list of requests, but having fellowship with God. When we pray, we enter into the life of the triune God (Ephesians 2:17–18). Our prayers are sometimes so pedestrian compared with the prayers of the New Testament where the emphasis is on knowing God and grasping his will (Ephesians 1:15–23; 3:14–19; Colossians 1:9–14). Prayer is hard work – sometimes it feels like we need to break the ice on our hearts each morning as we try to lift them up to God. However, prayer is vital to our spiritual health.

- *We need the encouragement of the local church.* Christian fellowship is the context in which Christian faith grows and reaches maturity (Hebrews 10:24–25). In the spiritual battle we need the support of our fellow combatants. We cannot survive for long without the regular communion we find among God's people.

Exercise: What helps you to read the Bible?

Here are some practical pointers that I have found helpful:

- Pray before, during and after you read the Bible.
- Always aim to feed your soul, not just inform your mind.
- Write down key thoughts in a notebook.

- Read long sections. Take a whole book of the Bible and spend a couple of hours reading it.
- Focus on short sections. Read a shorter section every day so that you can absorb its treasures.
- Meditate on Scripture. Take a short section and read and reread it. Write down a key verse on a piece of card and carry it with you. Pull it out in spare moments and turn it over in your mind.
- Be comprehensive. Don't confine your reading to the easier and more accessible parts of Scripture. Try to read the whole Bible at least once a year.
- Ask the right questions.
- Use the best Bible-reading aids available. l find the Bible Speaks Today series[2] an invaluable tool and I often use it in my personal devotions. What helps you?
- Get excited about the Bible – after all, this is God speaking!

What helps you to pray?

Here again are a few pointers:

- Use a prayer diary. I have one that runs for five days. I aim to pray through it at least once a week.
- Begin with worship. I have found that using a hymn book is incredibly helpful in focusing my heart on God.
- Find a prayer partner. Prayer should be both a private and a corporate experience. Having someone you can pray with adds discipline and strengthens prayer.
- Walk and pray. Most of my praying is done in the open air as I deliberately go for a prayer walk. But be careful – I once fell off a cliff because I was distracted!
- Use the prayers of the Bible. They are there to inspire and direct us. Look at the Psalms or Paul's recorded prayers.

- Always fuel your prayer with Scripture. Pray, read, pray, read, pray, read . . .
- Know yourself. What works best for you? For me it is praying early in the morning. When are you at your best? When is it easier to carve out time? When will you not be interrupted?
- Have special times. Devote a morning or a day to prayer.
- Remember what a great privilege prayer is. 'Prayer is telling God everything that is on your heart.'
- Persevere. Never, never, never, never, never give up.

Keep in step with the Spirit

The Christian life is not difficult – it is impossible. We can only live this way through the power that God miraculously imparts to us through the agency of his Spirit. The Spirit is a person, not a power. When he comes to dwell within us, he has an agenda, the agenda of transformation. He is actively at work, making us more like Jesus. The power that raised Christ from the dead is transforming us (Ephesians 1:18–23), imparting the power of life that is stronger than death.

We must attend to our relationship with the Spirit, not grieving him by our bitterness or quenching him by our unbelief. Our part is to come as empty vessels and ask for his grace and power to be poured into our lives. We are to be filled with the Spirit (Ephesians 5:18). This is not a polite suggestion, but a divine imperative. The command may be rendered as 'be being filled'. It is not a once and forever done deal, but a daily request. Each day we are to ask God to fill us with his Spirit and then walk in faith believing that God has answered our prayers. We bring the little beaker of our needy lives to the roaring Niagara of God's grace and find the strength we need to live a God-centred life. This fountain of life gives us all we need to conquer every sin, and power to vanquish every indulgence.

The battle will rage for the rest of our lives, but we should be experiencing ever-increasing victory.

Consider ferrets and rabbits

Do you remember our old farming friend from the beginning of the last chapter?

He came to preach one Pentecost Sunday and he spoke on Acts chapter 2. My wife and I had just moved from Birmingham. We had not yet got used to country ways. It was therefore slightly disconcerting when, in the middle of his sermon, he began to describe the change that the coming of the Spirit made on the early disciples: 'Before the Spirit came, the disciples were like rabbits, wasn't they? But after Pentecost they were more like ferrets! You know what I mean, don't you?'

Well no, actually. As a Brummie lad, all I knew about ferrets was that strange rustic people put them down their trousers.

So I asked him.

He was very kind, pitying my simplicity:

'You see, rabbits are very timid,' he told me. 'They will run a mile from the slightest sound. But ferrets are fearless. They are scared at nothing. If you put them down a hole, they will fight anything they meet. I've seen a ferret take on a badger. And the Holy Spirit changed the disciples and wants to change us.'

The 'trousering' of ferrets then seemed even more bizarre – if not positively insane – but at least the illustration now made sense.

The gift of the Spirit transformed Peter and the others, and it is supposed to transform us too. We face a lifelong battle with sin, but God has gifted us with his Spirit so that with his co-operation we can starve the old nature and feed the new, and so make slow but steady progress.

Questions

1. Read through the characteristics of the works of the flesh as listed in Galatians 5:19–21. How might these particular sins find expression today?

2. The devil is an expert at temptation. He has been doing it for a long time. Make a list of the temptations that he has designed particularly for you. What lessons have you learned in overcoming these?

3. Read these verses on the work of the Holy Spirit: Romans 8:5–11; Galatians 5:16–18; Ephesians 5:18. How does he help us to become holy?

4. According to Ephesians 4:29 – 5:2, how does our relationship with other people affect our relationship with the Holy Spirit?

5. Try honestly to answer these ten questions:

   - Do I read the Bible every day?
   - Do I regularly memorize and meditate on Scripture?
   - Do I work hard at consistent and focused prayer?
   - Do I pray for God to give me victory over sin?
   - Do I hate sin and regularly fight against it?
   - Do I exercise control in my use of social media?
   - Do I deliberately avoid situations in which I am susceptible to temptation?
   - Do I make sure that I get enough sleep and exercise and eat a balanced diet?
   - Do I keep 'short accounts with God', praying for forgiveness the moment I have failed?
   - Do I work hard at walking in the light in all my personal relationships?

8. Guard your marriage

Have you ever tried your hand at juggling?

Juggling is 'a physical skill involving the manipulation of objects for recreation, entertainment, art or sport'.[1] There is evidence that juggling goes back to at least 1,500 years before the birth of Christ. It was a common practice in many cultures, from the early Egyptians to the Meso-Americans, and from India to China. In Medieval Europe it was often frowned upon, since the church suspected that jugglers were men of low morals. Today it is a fairly common recreation as well as being an international 'sport'.

It's amazing what you can learn from Google!

But I have in mind a very specific feat. Have you ever tried to juggle a tennis ball, an orange and an egg? I have never seen it done, but I am told that it is particularly difficult because of the differing shapes and weights of the three objects. There is one simple rule for success – favour the egg! If you drop the tennis ball, it will bounce. If you spill the orange, it may get bruised, but it will survive. But if you drop the egg, it's game over.

Ministry often feels like juggling. You are trying to keep a lot of objects in the air at the same time. It needs concentration and skill and not a little perseverance. I have heard the ball / orange /

egg illustration applied to leadership in a quite specific way. Think of the tennis ball as your ministry, the orange as your ego and the egg as your marriage. If for some reason you have to leave a ministry you enjoy, it may be extremely painful, but you will survive. As long as we realize that ministry is a gift and we do not hold it too tightly, having to set it down will not be catastrophic. Like the tennis ball, we will bounce.

In these circumstances your ego may get bruised and you may take a while to recover, but recover you will. The orange is still edible.

But if you let your marriage slip and plummet, it can smash, and the consequences will be appalling. Ministry is for a while, but marriage is for life. Our leadership comes out of the context of our marital relationship. A healthy home is the necessary condition of a fruitful ministry. You can walk away from any ministry – you cannot walk away from your marriage.

And yet the tragedy is that so many leaders do. The pressures of service blind them to true biblical priorities. The job becomes a mistress, the home becomes a battleground, the kids become a distraction and the life is leeched out of a once-healthy marriage. We drop the egg, and all the king's horses and all the king's men cannot put it back together again.

The gift of singleness

This chapter is about guarding your marriage. However, it is important to recognize that not all of us are called to marriage or to the building of a Christian home. Writing to the Corinthians, Paul neither despises marriage nor derides singleness. There are distinct advantages in living a single life, particularly when it comes to the matter of Christian service (1 Corinthians 7). The single person is not distracted by the affairs of the world. He or she does not have to please a spouse, but can concentrate on pleasing God. Married people, on the other hand, will often find that they need to make difficult choices. They are not free to please themselves.

Single people sometimes complain that they are treated as second-class citizens. And often they are justified in their complaint. One of my friends at college applied for a job in a particular area of Christian ministry. During the interview one of his interrogators seemed fixated on the fact he was single: 'Are you sure there is no young lady on the horizon? How can you do the job without a wife? Can we trust you?' The last question was implied of course rather than stated. But the implications were clear: can a single man be trusted around members of the opposite sex? There may even have been an underlying doubt about his sexuality.

He never got the job.

This is tragic. Some of the greatest leaders of the church have been single. They have embraced their singleness and have seen it as a gift from God. Making full use of this gift has meant that they have been able to achieve great things for God. This was certainly the case with Paul.

If God has called you to singleness, remember that this has distinct advantages. It is a divine calling, and you should ask God to show you how you can take full advantage of it. Of course there will be particular pressures and stress points, but with the gift God will certainly give the grace to flourish in your singleness.

The demands of marriage

Getting married is like being executed. It is a joyful, fruitful and pleasant form of execution, but it is an execution nonetheless!

What do I mean?

Marriage involves the death of our old way of life. We are no longer single. (Obviously!) We can no longer please ourselves. The goal of my life is now to please another person. My dreams have to die so that new dreams can come to birth. My ambitions and preferences and passions must now be focused on the happiness of another. If I am a man, I am to love my wife as Christ loved the church, practically, purposefully, sacrificially and unto death. If I am a woman, I have to submit to my husband as the church submits to Christ, willingly, joyfully and deliberately (see 1 Peter 3:1–7). When preparing couples for marriage, I ask the man, 'Do you love this woman enough to die for her?' I ask the woman, 'Do you love this man enough to live for him?'

Describing marital love, the author of the Song of Solomon says,

> Place me like a seal over your heart,
> > like a seal on your arm;
> for love is as strong as death,
> > its jealousy unyielding as the grave.
> It burns like blazing fire,
> > like a mighty flame.
> Many waters cannot quench love;
> > rivers cannot sweep it away.
> If one were to give
> > all the wealth of one's house for love,
> > it would be utterly scorned.
> (Song of Solomon 8:6–7)

Look at the images. Love is as strong as death. You don't negotiate with death – it is powerful and uncompromising; it will have its way. And so will love. It blazes like a voracious fire, and everything melts in its heat. That is why the Bible is so insistent that it is only within the covenant of marriage – the lifelong commitment of one man and one woman – that the passions of love can be fully unleashed.

And that's only the start. Marriage involves a lifelong commitment to sacrificial love and joyful surrender. A good marriage is not like a sculpture which can be left. The sculptor puts a cloth over his masterpiece and goes away. When he returns and removes the cloth, it is as he left it. If you neglect the masterpiece of your marriage, however, when you take the cloth away, it will not be as you left it.

Marriage is more like a well-watered and wonderfully attended garden. It is the result of strenuous and exhausting labour. A beautiful garden is the result of long hours of unseen toil. The gardener is a man with blisters on his fingers and an ache in his bones. What happens if he neglects his work for a while? The garden will not be the same when he returns. It will be overrun with unwanted weeds. A neglected marriage will similarly descend into decay and disorder.

Marriages may be made in heaven – but the maintenance of the masterpiece is down to us.

We go through different phases in our lives, and in each new phase we have to learn to adapt our relationship to the prevailing conditions. So the relationship in the first flush of marital bliss is very different from when the home expands to include children. The empty nest is very different from the full nest. The years when career dominates are very different from the years of retirement and growing ill health.

Life changes. People change. And we too must change to adapt to new conditions within this most intimate of relationships. Marriages may be made in heaven – but the maintenance of the masterpiece is down to us.

Are you working hard to make your marriage flourish?

Marriage is difficult for everyone, but there are particular problems which threaten the marriages of Christian leaders.

Let me identify two of them.

Emotional detachment
The first is 'emotional detachment'.

If you are involved with people, then you will be involved in the totality of their lives. This means that you will rejoice when they rejoice and weep when they weep. And there is a lot of weeping in this poor fallen world. Everyone you meet is fighting a difficult battle. For some it seems as if the lights are about to go out. They feel alone in the valley of the shadow of death, and there are few comforting voices around them. God sends you to minister into that situation. You listen and love, and then speak. You cannot walk through that valley with them, but you can point them to Someone who can (Psalm 23:4). Our pastoral ministry always consists of this – pointing people to Jesus. We need to speak well of him, to magnify his sufficiency and to amplify his abundance. We do not want them to rely on us, but to depend on him.

But do people realize how exhausting this is?

I don't want to over-egg it, for many people work exceedingly hard and end the day exhausted. But there is a particular price to pay when God uses us to be channels of his grace into the broken lives of shattered people.

Then there is the shepherding of conflict and the management of change – often the same thing! No wonder Paul complained of the pressure of all the churches.

Sometimes it is far more prosaic. It may be the demands of climbing the hill one more time to deliver a message on the doubtful reading of an obscure text in a minor prophet. It may be yet another discipleship class or a course in marriage preparation or a group of Sunday school kids who, Bart-Simpson-style, will come up with the most obscure questions ever invented by the human mind. It may be yet another protracted or tedious or challenging meeting with our fellow leaders.

And all the time we have to behave as leaders should behave. We expend huge amounts of emotional energy, and when we are finished, all our emotional reserves are exhausted.

Going home
Let me describe the scenario. I have been attending a long and exhausting elders' meeting. The outcome has been good, but

the journey there was painful. We had to talk about the difficulties in staffing the Sunday school, a letter from an irate church member who thinks we have been singing too many new songs, an equally emphatic epistle from someone else who thinks that our music is stuck in the past, the painful news of a failed marriage, the joyful news of a new conversion, the challenge of meeting our budget and the threat of resignation from our church caretaker. We have talked and prayed together. We haven't always agreed, but have worked hard on the cultivation of unity. The meeting has lasted longer than expected, and when I get in, my wife has been anxiously watching the clock for the past hour.

The conversation runs something like this:

'Was it a good meeting?'

'Yes, I suppose so.'

'You don't sound sure?'

'Yes, it was great. The best meeting we've ever had!'

'Are you being sarcastic?'

'No . . . well, yes, just a bit.'

'What did you discuss?'

'You know . . .'

'I don't. That's why I am asking.'

'The usual stuff.'

'What usual stuff?'

'I don't know – the usual stuff. What we always discuss . . .'

'Did you come to some big decisions?'

'Yes.'

'What?'

'You know . . .'

'I don't!'

'Oh, I don't know – I just can't be bothered to say. Have we got something to eat . . . ?'

It's not a matter of confidentiality. It's not that she doesn't need to know. The bottom line is that I am emotionally drained and cannot face another debate. When it comes to this wonderfully

loyal woman with whom I have chosen to share my life and
ministry, I just cannot be bothered to expend the emotional
energy necessary to enter into a conversation that is anything
other than superficial.

And sometimes it's even worse
It's my day off. We are in the car, driving out to get coffee
somewhere. I am musing on the pastoral issues I am facing at
the moment. Then my wife speaks and her words send a chill
through my bones. They are the most terrifying words in the
English language:
  'Why are you quiet? Talk to me!'
  'What do you want me to talk about?'
  'Anything.'
  'Albion did well on Saturday.'
  'Not football.'
  'Oh, I don't know. Why don't you talk to me? I'll just listen . . .'
And so it goes on.
  She needs support or encouragement or reassurance, and I
have nothing to give. My emotional resources are expended.
  I am not only her husband; I am also her pastor. Who else can
she turn to?
  So rule number one: make sure that you have emotional
reserves for your partner. It is hypocritical to be the most sensitive
and emotionally attuned pastor/youth group leader/evangelist
outside the home, while inside it you are just about as useful as
a Toblerone toast rack. Your partner should have the first call on
your sympathy and understanding. It may seem noble to be
spent in the service of others, but this is not what God wants if
there is nothing in reserve for your spouse.
  And there is a second problem.

Misdirected anger
As I said earlier, I have always held a surgery on Wednesday
mornings. I had been a pastor for about a year when one

Wednesday morning I had three visitors in quick succession. I'm pretty sure that it wasn't a conspiracy, but they were all fairly critical of my leadership. I cannot remember the details, but I recall that two of them didn't like my preaching and one of them thought that I was trying to take the church in the wrong direction.

How did I react?

Although I say it myself, I was magnificent!

I wasn't defensive. I listened to the criticisms and agreed that I had a long way to go. I never raised my voice. I was calm and cool and collected. I remembered that somewhere in the Bible it said that 'a gentle answer turns away wrath' (see Proverbs 15:1), and so I gave them the gentlest answer they had ever received. They were placated, and the visits ended with prayer. The situation was defused, and I felt the satisfaction of a job well done.

I walked home feeling the warm glow that comes from the successful negotiation of a potentially hazardous journey.

It was lunchtime when I got in.

'What do you want for lunch?' my wife enquired.

Now I've always had a soft spot for beans on toast – they are my number-one comfort food.

'After the morning I have had, I'd love beans on toast,' I replied.

'Oh, I'm sorry – I forgot to get any. You can have tinned tomatoes instead.'

I went ballistic! How can you run a house unstocked with Mr Heinz's most famous product? What is life without the glorious fruit of the haricot plant – *Phaseolus vulgaris* – stewed in a rich tomato sauce and carefully preserved in that familiar blue tin?

I was very angry, and I made sure that my wife knew about it.

I had been raging for a few minutes when I saw that she was in tears. What a beast! How vile can a man be?

I seated her on my lap and apologized profusely. I begged her forgiveness.

We sorted it out. She went and bought some beans. Peace was restored.

Good and bad anger

I don't think that it was until the next day that I began to analyse what had happened. My anger may have been justified; it had just chosen the wrong target. Anger is not always wrong. It becomes wrong when it takes control or it is misdirected. As I look back, I think that my three morning callers may have had some grounds for the criticism they channelled towards me. However, the approach of at least one of them was ungracious, and potentially destructive of a young man at the beginning of his ministry. I thought that turning the other cheek meant agreeing with their assessment and not defending myself. I'm not sure that that was right. I may well have been justified at feeling a little cross with the unjustified criticism. However, my real mistake was to feel anger, drive it down and then pick a vulnerable victim on whom to vent it.

We do this all the time. In public we behave as we think a Christian leader should do, but in private we allow our frustrations and irritations to overflow against the people closest to us. It may be your spouse. It may be your kids. In either case, it is misdirected and destructive.

What makes us behave like this? I think that it is a mixture of misunderstanding and cowardice.

Firstly, misunderstanding: we have misunderstood the nature of leadership. It is right to be meek. As leaders, we are not to assert our rights and demand personal allegiance which supersedes allegiance to Christ. We must never seek to control or manipulate the consciences of the people we lead. But this does not mean that we become doormats and absorb every criticism without an answer. Read the Gospels and you see that Jesus often confronted hypocrisy and cant. He threw the moneylenders out of the temple and was far from complimentary about the Pharisees (Matthew 21:12–17; 23:1–39). Read the Epistles and you will see Paul doing the same. On one occasion he confronted Peter because of his duplicity (Galatians 2:11–21).

Taken in the right way, some criticism can be incredibly productive. If we are always defensive, we may fail to learn the lessons which constructive criticism can bring. But not all criticism is constructive. Some is unfair and misguided, and some positively toxic. It is not our role to absorb it without answer. If we do so, our critics go away confirmed in their views and will feel justified in doing the same thing again to some other poor unsuspecting leader.

We feel hurt and angry and hard done by. And with all those negative emotions washing around inside us, we can so easily vent them on the people we are closest to. Sometimes it is as blatant as my baked-bean debacle. But usually it is subtler. We are out of sorts or moody or withdrawn. The toxic emotions are released into the home, and the innocent suffer.

The second reason why we react like this is cowardice: we are afraid of asserting the truth and challenging ungodly views. We pick on our family members because they are an easy target and won't hit back.

Grow a backbone!

Lessons along the way

I have a wife who is practically perfect in every way – I'm afraid that I don't quite match up. However, over more than thirty years of marriage and full-time Christian ministry we have learned several lessons:

Agree together to put God first. When I proposed to my wife, we had been courting for five years, so she knew me pretty well. 'I want you to marry me, but I have to tell you that you will always be the second person in my life. God has to come first and, what is more, I think he is calling me into full-time service.' Not the most romantic proposal ever – but at least it was honest! 'Of course the answer is yes,' she replied, 'and I want God to be first as well.'

We married six months later. And here is what we have learned: the closer we are to God, the closer we are to each other. Marriage is like a pyramid. God is at the summit, and husband and wife are at two corners. As they travel upwards towards God, they get closer to each other.

Recognize that marriage involves very hard work. There is no such thing as a conflict-free marriage. The idea of a 'perfect partner' or a 'soulmate' is unbiblical, unrealistic and positively destructive. Take two sinful people and expose them to each other in the most intimate relationship imaginable and you're lighting the blue touch paper – stand back and wait for fireworks. How could it be otherwise? In public you may get away with wearing a leadership mask for some time, but it won't work at home. There is nowhere to hide. So recognize that this is your fundamental relationship and work hard to cultivate it.

Keep short accounts and 'don't let the sun go down on your wrath.'[2] One summer I worked for an Anglican vicar in a delightful mining community in North Yorkshire. He allowed me to sit in on several marriage preparation courses. He always gave the couples one piece of advice that I will never forget. In a broad Yorkshire accent he would say, 'Never let sun go down on't wrath.' When we rub up against each other, there may be times when passions run high. You will fall out. But don't blow up, and don't clam up. Deal with issues as soon as you can. Never leave anything until the next day.

Don't allow ministry to become your mistress. We love our service for God. If we don't, it is doubtful whether we are in the right place. But the moment that ministry becomes our first love, we are in trouble. I have heard wives complain about this. 'I feel so guilty. I know how committed my husband is. I don't want to discourage him. If it were another woman, it would be clearer, but how do you compete with the church?' In case I have not underlined it sufficiently, here is the fundamental message of this chapter: your marriage takes precedence over your ministry. This is the biblical order. We neglect it at our peril. Set boundaries around your marriage to protect it.

Pray together. Prayer is difficult, as we've seen already. We need all the help we can get. When we marry, God gives us a prayer partner for life. My wife knows me. She knows the things that faze me and the battles that I fight. She is my most faithful supporter in prayer – I call her my secret weapon. Together we pray for our family and for our ministry. We also pray about our marriage. It is difficult to continue arguing with someone with whom you are praying. When we pray with anyone, we are exposing ourselves before the God who is light and in whom there is no darkness at all (1 John 1:5–7). In this way, we walk in the light with each other.

Recognize the importance of sex. God invented sex. It is good. But it is also dangerous. That is why he confined it to marriage. We quoted from the Song of Solomon earlier. This is neither a detailed allegory nor an ancient sex manual. It is a celebration of the importance of sexual union between husband and wife. Sex is like the oil that we put into the engines of our cars. It is a relatively small ingredient, but watch what happens when it is absent. The self-surrender, which is the foundation of sexual intercourse, is the most intimate form of personal communication that two human beings are capable of. It is the oil that lubricates the engine of marriage. When sex is good, most things will be working well in the marriage.

Communicate, communicate, communicate. Within marriage we must practise truth and transparency. Truth may be painful, but untruth will destroy a marriage. In my first church we had a farmer who worked extraordinarily long hours. He told me that every day he would come home at 10 am for a late breakfast. He had been out and about since 5 am. After eating, he would sit in the kitchen with his wife on his lap, and they would talk together for at least half an hour. It kept their relationship strong and intimate. There are of course many forms of communication, but creating time every day to talk is vital. And never forget the power of words. Paul warns the Ephesians about the danger they pose (Ephesians 4:29). They can be 'corrupting' – a word sometimes used to describe rotten fruit. They can contaminate any relationship and remain as an indelible stain unless they are dealt with. The old saying that 'words can never hurt me' is completely erroneous. Use words to heal rather than to harm.

Forgive and keep no record of wrongs. A successful marriage is the union of two good forgivers. Two imperfect people will constantly need the gift of forgiveness. Before you look at what Christ expects of you, concentrate on what he has done for you. Remember that there is forgiveness for those who fail. Dwell on the fact that he has given us the rich supply of the Holy Spirit to enable us to live for God's glory. Don't forget that God is committed to you, and he is also committed to your marriage.

Deal with toxic emotions. Some marriages are marred by venomous emotions like bitterness, rage, anger, slander and malice (Ephesians 4:30–31). We have to learn to give our emotions the right place and prevent them from turning toxic. Paul warns that such passions will grieve the Holy Spirit. They are also destructive to a healthy marriage.

Magnify grace. One of the natural tendencies of the human heart is to descend into legalism. Somehow we think that our acceptance with God depends on our performance. But it is only as we discover God's extravagant and unconditional grace towards his people that we are able to function in a healthy way. And the same is true in our marriage relationship. Grace is to be the basis of marital bliss. Grace keeps no record of wrongs. In Paul's words, '[Love] always protects, always trusts, always hopes, always perseveres. Love never fails' (1 Corinthians 13:7–8). Dwell on the fact that God has given us the rich supply of the Holy Spirit to enable us to live for his glory. Don't forget that God is committed to you and also to your marriage. As we look to him and draw on his strength, we will find all the help we need to be what we are meant to be.

We really can do all things through Christ who strengthens us (Philippians 4:13).

What about the kids?

Bringing up children in today's world demands wisdom, grace, perseverance and a good sense of humour. At every stage there is a new challenge. From the moment the midwife places this tiny squalling cosmos in your arms until the end of your life, you have inherited this glorious gift.

I once heard an interview with a woman who was celebrating her hundredth birthday. She was as sharp as a whip. When they asked her what life was like, she said, 'I can't do what I used to. But life is so much easier since I got my seventy-three-year-old son into a care home . . . he's such a tearaway!'

As I've said, it's a lifelong commitment!

This is obviously a vitally important subject and probably deserves another book in itself, but here are some thoughts from Edrie's and my experience and observations. (There's also a list of suggested titles in the 'Further reading' section at the end of this book.)

Guard your home. Protect your children from the pressures, disappointments and conflicts of leadership, and be careful about what you expose your kids to. When church is tough, you will need to be honest and open – they will soon see through any deception. But be careful that you do not draw them into a situation that they don't have the maturity to cope with. If you are always critical of church and other Christians, they too will develop a critical attitude.

Remember that your kids are only kids, so allow them to grow up and don't pressurize them. There is no biblical office of 'PK' (i.e. pastor's kid). They are just normal kids, and both you and your congregation need to know this. I remember a young couple who settled in our church. They were about to start a family, and the woman confided in my wife, 'We like it here because your kids are just as naughty as everybody else's.' (Is that a compliment?)

Remember that as a leader you are meant to be a model parent. This does not mean that your kids are meant to be model kids. One of the testing grounds of leadership is the home (1 Timothy 3:7; Titus 1:5–9). Leaders have to govern their homes well. Their children must not be wild and unruly. Yet you don't have to be a *perfect* parent – such an animal doesn't exist. You are supposed to do the job in such a way that you can model parenting to others in the church. The members of your congregation need to learn that your children are not meant to be perfect. And so do you. Avoid saying things like, 'I am the pastor – you are letting me down!' That borders on manipulation.

Treat them with respect. Keep your word. If you have promised to spend time with them, don't allow leadership commitments to distract you. You may feel guilty about having to reschedule a deacons' meeting or rearrange an appointment, but your kids need to see that they can trust you and that you don't always put your ministry ahead of them.

Don't embarrass them. Be careful about what you say about them in public. If you want to use a family illustration in a sermon, ask their permission before doing so. Remember how embarrassing it is for a teenager to have one of his parents upfront.

Do not provoke your children to anger (Ephesians 6:4; Colossians 3:21). When they were growing up, those were my kids' favourite Bible verses! You need to know your children well enough to understand what makes them angry. Avoid things like favouritism, over-indulgence and over-protectiveness.

Use kind, gracious and loving discipline. You will have to work out what sort of discipline you are comfortable with, but the Bible is clear that good parents love their kids enough to teach them the difference between right and wrong, and to enforce the lesson with appropriate sanctions (Hebrews 12:5–11). Your kids need to understand that disobedience has consequences, and that there is a connection between sin and pain.

Remember that you will make mistakes. Don't be afraid to say sorry and ask for your children's forgiveness. Almost every parent I know has at some time asked the question: 'Where did we go wrong?' Sometimes parenting feels like blundering along from one crisis to another. Guilt is almost an occupational hazard. The only answer I know is to keep on seeking God's forgiveness and wisdom every day, and then to leave our children in his hands.

Tell them that you love them. Tell them constantly and let them see that you love them without strings attached. You want them to shape up and fly right, but they will need to see that your love is not conditioned upon their performance or conformity to the rules. Pray through the description of love in 1 Corinthians 13:4–7. Do you love your spouse and children like this? Model God's love to them and let them flourish under your good pleasure.

Remember how quickly time goes and don't wish it away. A pastor once told me that he had asked the older members of his congregation what three pieces of advice they would give to new parents. The gathered wisdom was far-ranging and sometimes contradictory! However, the one thing shared by almost all the older parents was this: 'Sleepless nights are exhausting, toddlers are demanding, school years can be difficult, and teenagers are impossible! But when you are tempted to wish away those early years, remember how quickly they pass and remind yourself that you can never get them back. Enjoy them and make the most of them.'

Most of all try to win your children's hearts for Christ. Pray for them to be converted and teach them about the grace of God. Don't just teach grace – live it out before them. Be careful of turning them into little Pharisees who obey your rules but don't know Jesus. Remember that only God can actually change their hearts – it is a divine prerogative. Give them back to him and trust them to his gracious care.

Give them roots and wings. Live out your faith before them and teach them the Bible. Teach them that the natural response to a crisis is to pray, and show them that God is a reality in your life. But when the time comes, let them go; don't be either overprotective or overindulgent. When they leave home, entrust them to God. Don't try to control them at a distance.

Questions

1. What are the advantages of singleness in Christian service? What are the 'particular pressures and stress points'?
2. How is marriage like execution?

3. What steps could you take to reserve emotional energy for your marriage relationship?

4. How do you deal with anger in a godly way?

5. Discuss the 'Lessons along the way' with your spouse. Are there any of them that resonate particularly? Come up with a list of three things that you can do together as a result of reading this chapter.

6. Ephesians 4:25 – 5:2 is about dealing with conflicts within the church. What can we learn from this passage about the way in which we deal with conflict within our marriages?

7. Look at the section: 'What about the kids?' Repeat the same exercise as in question 5 above.

9. Build godly relationships

Eb and Flo

Everyone needs a good mentor. My first experience of mentoring in ministry came from a man who would never have cast himself in that role.

Ebenezer Knight was in his mid-70s when I was in my mid-20s. I had been in ministry for less than a year; he had served the same church for most of his lifetime. Apart for a brief pastorate in the USA, Eb had been the pastor of a small Baptist church in Wiltshire for decades. He had been married to Florence for all of that time, and they were affectionately referred to as 'Eb and Flo'!

In the early days of my ministry we could not afford to run a car, and so Eb would regularly drive me to meetings where pastors and church leaders got together for mutual encouragement. I was very grateful, and the wisdom that he imparted during those journeys was invaluable. Travelling along the narrow, winding Wiltshire lanes, I would ask a question, and he would answer it from his deep reserves of hard-won wisdom. As he did so, he would sometimes take his eyes off the road and fix me with a kindly look. I was slightly torn – his insights were invaluable, but his lack of attention to the direction of the car was somewhat distracting! However, the angels must have been watching over us because we never crashed.

One Wednesday afternoon I asked Eb's advice on a question that had been troubling me for a while: 'Can a pastor have friends?'

I had heard someone say that being a minister was lonely, and you could not build lasting friendships either inside or outside the church.

Eb didn't answer for a while. When he turned to me, I was amazed to see tears in his eyes. This was a first.

'When I started in ministry, that was the advice I was given,' he confided. 'For twenty years I followed it. I avoided strong friendships because I thought that this was what pastors were supposed to do. But it was bad advice. It's not easy being a pastor. You need friends, and if God gives them to you, receive them as a very valuable gift.'

The danger of individualism

I have never forgotten Eb's words.

One of the dangers in Christian leadership is the temptation towards individualism. Most leaders have a sense of vision and direction, and want to move people from where they are to where they could be. That's why they're in leadership. But this sometimes comes with a good dose of individualism.

John Oswald Sanders (1902–92) was General Director of Overseas Missionary Fellowship (then known as China Inland Mission) in the 1950s and 1960s. He wrote more than forty books on the Christian life. After he retired, he became an elder statesman and pastor to pastors throughout the world. In 1967 he wrote a book called *Spiritual Leadership* which is worth its weight in gold. It was the first book on leadership that I read after I had been called to ministry. However, on a few points I have come to disagree with Sanders.

In a chapter called 'The Cost of Leadership', for example, he lists one of the challenges as the danger of loneliness:

> From its very nature, the lot of the leader must be a lonely one. He must always be ahead of his followers. Though he be the friendliest of men, there are areas of his life in which he must be prepared to tread a lonely path. The fact dawned on Dixon E. Hoste when Hudson Taylor laid down the direction of the China Inland Mission and appointed Hoste his successor. After the interview during which the appointment was made, the new leader, sensible to the weight of responsibility which was now his, said, 'And now I have no one, no one but God!' In his journey to the top he had left behind all his contemporaries and stood alone in the mount with his God.[1]

It was these words that had spooked me and caused me to consult Eb. This was a popular view when I started out in leadership. It seemed both biblical and a little romantic. Sanders alluded to the example of Moses who met with God in the solitude of the mountain and then led the people to the edge of the land of promise. Here surely is an example of the kind of rugged individualism that we should model ourselves on. He also referred to Enoch who walked with God for 300 years before God took him to heaven (Genesis 5:21–24), and Jonah who was alone in his ministry to Nineveh. Paul was alone at the end of his life (2 Timothy 1:15). Sanders quotes A. W. Tozer: 'Most of the world's great souls have been lonely. Loneliness is the price of sainthood.'[2]

There is something a little appealing to the human ego about leadership in such individualistic terms. We read the biographies of great men and women, and are perhaps persuaded that their greatness was the result of their loneliness. Many leaders are self-starters. They easily become impatient with others who cannot move at the same pace.

It may be that circumstances and opposition force us into isolation. We should certainly seek to foster a personal relationship with God which can only be done in secret – 'on the mountain alone' in a sense. However, the idea of deliberately freezing out friendships is neither healthy nor biblical.

People need people

I once heard a sermon entitled 'When God is not enough'. I think that this was deliberately provocative – a preacher's opening gambit to secure the attention of his congregation. Nonetheless, the speaker pressed his point home.

He began with Genesis 2:18. God had created a faultless world in which everything was perfect and complete (1:31). Adam found himself living in a flawless environment. However, as God gazes on the world he has created for the first time, he recognizes that something is missing: 'The LORD God said, "It is not good for the man to be alone. I will make a helper suitable for him"' (Genesis 2:18).

And so the Lord creates the woman to be a partner who will complete the man and act as a 'suitable helper' (2:20). By naming the animals, the man has become aware of his solitary state – they have mates but he has none. When he names the woman, he affirms that here is a being who, although different, is at the same time physically and emotionally and intellectually as he is (2:23). In this event in Eden we see not only the creation of the first marriage and the first family, but also the first community. It is not good for this man to be alone. It is not good for any man or woman to be alone. It is not good for any Christian leader to be alone.

People need people.

Behind this commitment to partnership lies the fact that God is Trinity. The one eternal God has always existed in a sublime, loving relationship of three Persons. It is not good for God to be alone if by this we mean that he is to exist in splendid isolation with no eternal, internal and infinite relationship of love. Such a God has never existed.

And we humans have been made in the image of God (Genesis 1:26–28). Relationships are necessary to our well-being.

This was the sense in which the preacher used the text. Surely God is always enough for us? Weren't we created to know and enjoy him? What more could we possibly need? And yet it is God himself who recognizes a need and provides the solution. The man needs the woman, and the woman needs the man, if together they are to fulfil their creation mandate of populating the earth (1:28). But they need each other for other reasons too. In the words of the Book of Common Prayer, 'It [marriage] was ordained for the mutual society, help, and comfort, that the one ought to have of the other, both in prosperity and adversity.'

Relationships are necessary to our well-being.

There's an old song which says that people who need people are the luckiest people in the world. But would it not be more accurate to say that they are the *only* people in the world? We were made with an inbuilt need for friendship. We cannot function properly without it. Our relationships define us.

This is certainly true when we become Christians. Salvation is personal – but it is never private. In John Wesley's words, 'There is nothing more unchristian than a solitary Christian.'[3]

Before we go on, perhaps we need a word of warning. Like any gift that God gives us, there are potential dangers. Friendship can be misused. We must never turn it into an idol. Loving God has to come first. And as leaders, we must be very careful that friendships with certain church members are not perceived as favouritism. And never forget that the desire to be friendly can lead us into misunderstandings with members of the opposite sex. An overly warm or familiar relationship can be misinterpreted. Be careful about the tone of your text messages. Avoid private meetings that may be compromising. Remember the dangerous potential of unwise touch. Recognize that shared intimacies, even in a pastoral setting, can lead to unforeseen dangers. Speaking personally, I make it a rule never to see members of the opposite sex on my own and have never flirted with anyone other than my wife.

Leaders need friends

I believe that friendship is particularly necessary for those who find themselves in positions of leadership.

A married leader enjoys the partnership of a spouse. There may be matters of confidentiality which have to be observed, but they are fewer than we might sometimes imagine. Before people offer to disclose the intimate details of their lives to me, I will always tell them that I keep no secrets from my wife. I respect her advice and covet her prayers. I may want to protect her from some things, but I will usually be as transparent with her as I can.

But the Bible is clear that there are other levels of appropriate friendship too which are necessary for spiritual health and vital to success in ministry. Indeed, the Bible has a profound and often neglected theology of friendship.

Consider the teaching of Jesus:

> My command is this: love each other as I have loved you.
> Greater love has no one than this: to lay down one's life for one's friends. You are my friends if you do what I command. I no longer call you servants, because a servant does not know his master's business. Instead, I have called you friends, for everything that I learned from my Father I have made known to you.
> (John 15:12–15)

Jesus sought friendship and offered it and demonstrated it. Today he proves to be the best and most faithful friend we can have. Here is the friend who goes out into the darkness of separation from God – into the deepest and most profound loneliness that can be imagined. He does this so that those who trust him as Saviour and friend will never know this final desertion for themselves.

The book of Proverbs is replete with teaching on the nature of friendship. It tells us just how important it is. Friendship leads to safety (Proverbs 11:14), and comfort in adversity (17:17). It is the source of wisdom (19:20; 24:6), and the means that God uses to sharpen us up (27:17). How do we find such friends? Proverbs directs us in this also (12:26; 13:20; 14:6–7; 22:24–25).

And then of course we have those wonderful examples of friendship described in the Bible. We think of Ruth and Naomi (Ruth 1:16–17) or David and Jonathan (1 Samuel 18:1–3). When Elijah's faith seemed to collapse and he lamented his isolation and loneliness, part of God's solution was to give him Elisha, a companion who would ensure that he would never be alone again (2 Kings 2:2).

In the New Testament the same pattern emerges. Jesus created a team and invested time in them. It is clear that he knew it would take a team of people to build his church. He sent out his disciples two by two. This was partly because of the need for two voices to give a credible witness, but also because of the need for mutual support and encouragement.

Paul and Barnabas, the first missionaries, worked as a team (Acts 13 – 14). In fact, this was always Paul's method of operation. He invested a lot of time in creating teams and training fellow workers. He was concerned with the preparation of a new generation of Christian workers, and instructed Timothy to find faithful men who could perpetuate the ministry which he had begun (2 Timothy 2:2). But his concern was not only with the future; he felt the need for support and encouragement in the present.

When Paul wrote 2 Timothy, he knew that he was approaching the end of his life (2 Timothy 4:6). He was comforted by a clean conscience and certain hope (4:7–8). He also knew that when there was no human support, the Lord stood by him (4:17). However, what was also abundantly clear in the last chapter was how much Paul depended on people:

> Do your best to come to me quickly, for Demas, because he loved this world, has deserted me and has gone to Thessalonica. Crescens has gone to Galatia, and Titus to Dalmatia. Only Luke is with me. Get Mark and bring him with you, because he is helpful to me in my ministry. I sent Tychicus to Ephesus. When you come, bring the cloak that I left with Carpus at Troas, and my scrolls, especially the parchments.
> (4:9–13)

Can you feel the pathos? Paul is grieved that his friend Demas has deserted him. Crescens, Titus and Tychicus have been sent away on important apostolic missions, but this has left Paul bereft. Doctor Luke is still there, and Paul urges Timothy and Mark to come as soon as possible.

If we picture Paul as a rugged individualist – a kind of self-sufficient heroic pioneer – then these words should make us think again. Here is a vulnerable man who will press on and be faithful no matter what the cost. If he is forced to be alone, he will trust in God to support him, but he will not like it. Almost his last recorded words are an appeal to his friends to come and help him.

Band of Brothers

Have you ever seen the HBO mini-series *Band of Brothers*? It is the story of 'Easy' Company, a group of soldiers who are part of the 506th Parachute Infantry Regiment, US Army 101st Airborne Division. It describes their mission in Europe from

D-Day to the end of the Second World War.[4] Of course the title comes from the famous St Crispin's Day speech in Shakespeare's play *Henry V*. Adversity creates companionship, which is stronger than the ties of blood or social standing.

CNN's Paul Clinton said that the series was 'a remarkable testament to that generation of citizen soldiers, who responded when called upon to save the world for democracy and then quietly returned to build the nation that we now all enjoy, and all too often take for granted'.[5]

The mutual commitment of the men, their loving sacrifice and their devotion to the task in hand are what make the series so powerful. The strapline on the posters read: 'All we knew was that we were in this together.'

I watched this at a time when the church I was leading was going through difficulties. What helped us through was the fact that we had a leadership team that felt like a band of brothers.

Every year we would take a couple of days away to pray and strategize. When we returned, we would justify our absence by setting out clear areas of direction and development for the year ahead. However, as I look back on those times of reflection, it seems to me that the most valuable outcome was the way in which we were bound together as a group of leaders. We got to see one another away from the pressures of church life. We prayed for one another and talked about our kids. We developed a level of transparency which could only be cultivated in a more informal setting. In the *annus horribilis* mentioned above we spent the morning praying and the afternoon tenpin bowling.

Not very spiritual?

For this group of leaders, it was exactly what we needed. We were able to reflect on the pressures of leadership and rejoice that God had given us one another. We were able to step outside our situation and laugh together. We now had a firm foundation for the tough decisions we had to face in the future. I came away thankful to God that he had given me these guys to work with, and I was convinced that I should do everything in my power to cultivate our relationships and deepen our friendships.

Wisdom in numbers

There should always be a plurality of leaders in the local church. Whenever the apostles set up new churches, they appointed a group of elders to serve it (Acts 14:23). This seems to be a common pattern (Philippians 1:1; Titus 1:5). There may be a leader among leaders. Peter takes the lead in Acts (Acts 2:14; 3:1), and Paul recognizes that some leaders will be set aside for full-time ministry of the Word (1 Timothy 5:17–18). Regular pulpit ministry will give authority, since much of leadership comes through preaching and teaching.

However, it seems to me that this does not mean that one full-time leader should exercise authority over and above the team he leads. A team of leaders gives support and balance and mutual encouragement. And apart from the fact that this is the biblical model, there are many reasons to be committed to team ministry:

- It recognizes the fact that we have different strengths and weaknesses.
- It acts as a check and a source of wisdom.
- It militates against spiritual pride.
- It multiplies ministries.
- It leads to more effective pastoral care as this is shared.
- It enables the pastor to concentrate on his core ministries.
- It prolongs the pastor's ministry – he is supported and encouraged.
- It prepares for the future – the church does not fail if one leader falls.

Encouragement

Encouragement has been described as 'the oxygen of the soul'. Life is tough. The Christian life is demanding. And leadership carries its own demands. Most of the people you meet every day are in need of encouragement. Unfortunately, we can all come to church feeling pretty low and, after a verbal pounding, leave feeling even worse. The unofficial motto of the French Foreign Legion is: 'If I falter, push me on; if I stumble, pick me up; if I retreat, shoot me.' I suspect that it is the unofficial pastoral policy of many churches too – in practice if not in theory. We shoot our wounded!

How many mistakes have I made as a Christian leader? Too many to mention. How often have I felt inadequate for the task? Often. How many times has a demanding Sunday been followed by a deflated and depressing Monday? Frequently.

What has kept me going? The faithfulness of God, the love of a good woman and the regular encouragement of godly friends.

There are some people who have a particular gift of encouragement. They are worth their weight in gold. However, the Christian church is supposed to be a community of encouragement. We need to belong to a nurturing Christian community:

> And let us consider how we may spur one another on towards love and good deeds, not giving up meeting together, as some are in the habit of doing, but encouraging one another – and all the more as you see the Day approaching.
> (Hebrews 10:24–25)

Christians need to be together. We must not opt out of regular fellowship. Life is hectic, so we can always find good reasons not to meet with our fellow Christians, but this will inevitably lead to spiritual decline. The coal has to be in the middle of the fire to retain its heat. If it is removed to the hearth, it will soon become cold and lifeless.

For three years I served in a ministry beyond the local church. This meant that I was often on the road, visiting other churches for one month in four. My fellow leaders were great. They told me to leave the church in their hands and not to worry about things like leaders' meetings or home groups. I should be free to concentrate on travelling. This was great in theory, and I certainly trusted the guys to do a good job. But what I discovered after the first month of being absent from the church was that I was missing my Christian family like crazy. I couldn't work out why I felt so disconnected and jaded. I needed to be with the people I loved; I needed the church.

And what are we supposed to do when we attend church? Hebrews tells us that we are to go with a definite agenda. We are to consider why we are there. The word suggests that we have a purpose and goal. We go to give, not to take. We are to give encouragement, so that our fellow Christians feel affirmed in their faith and inspired towards love and good deeds.

Encouragement involves using words that build up, so that recipients want to be more passionate followers of Jesus Christ. We encourage them by pointing them to God. We want to help them to have confidence in him and to trust in his promises so that they can be bold in living out their faith and effective in fulfilling their ministry.

Accountability

If we are to remain fresh in ministry, we will need a regular spiritual check-up. The problem is that we are not always good at assessing ourselves and diagnosing our true spiritual condition. This is why Proverbs says,

> Wounds from a friend can be trusted,
>   but an enemy multiplies kisses.
> (27:6)

Psalm 141:5 says something similar:

> Let a righteous man strike me – that is a kindness;
>> let him rebuke me – that is oil on my head.
> My head will not refuse it,
>> for my prayer will still be against the deeds of evildoers.

Do you have such a friend? What is needed is an intentional relationship of trust in which we can be open and honest and accountable. We are not talking here about a return to the old idea of the 'confessional'. We can confess our sins to God, and he will forgive us. We do not need a person to absolve us. However, what we do need is someone we can trust who will be committed to us in love. This person will ask us the questions we are uncomfortable about answering. They will pray with us and for us. They will hold us accountable and tell us the truth, no matter how uncomfortable that truth might be. They will be more concerned for the health of our souls than for the temporary ease of our minds. They will want to know about our relationship with God and with our families and with our fellow leaders. They will enquire about our prayer life and our Bible reading. What battles with sin are we currently fighting? What are our victories and defeats? What are we afraid of? What challenges us and what thrills us? Do we have unresolved conflicts? How is our work and our rest and our play?

Is it uncomfortable to develop such a relationship? Yes. Is it dangerous? It can be. It can become unhealthy and prurient. There are some things that should be reserved for discussion between husband and wife alone. An unwholesome dependence may develop. It may turn into a confessional, even if we don't want it to.

But is it worth the risk? I think so. With the right friend and the right degree of openness, there can be a regular spiritual check-up that would otherwise be missing.

Staying fresh is a painful and demanding exercise. If we are to manage it, we will need friends who can spur us on and hold us accountable.

When we consider the blessings of God – the gifts that add beauty and joy to our lives, that enable us to keep going through stretches of boredom and even suffering – friendship is very near the top.[6]

Questions

1. Why is individualism so attractive? What are the results of rampant individualism in Christian ministry?
2. What are the dangers of friendship that we must be aware of?
3. Look up the verses from Proverbs about friendship on page 133. What do they tell us about the nature of friendship?
4. How do we inspire our fellow Christians towards love and good deeds?
5. Why is building an accountability relationship uncomfortable? Why can it be dangerous? Why is it important?
6. What are the blessings of friendship?

10. Preach the gospel to your own heart

When I began my ministry, I remember that I was amazed and excited and afraid all at the same time. I was idealistic and wanted to be the best I could be for God. At the same time, I had a sense of unworthiness because of the gap between the ideals to which I aspired and the daily reality of the battle against sin.

At my first church, I would take a long walk each Sunday morning as I prepared my heart to preach. Sometimes the sins and errors and failures of the previous week would just sweep over me. A little voice would whisper in my ear, 'What a hypocrite you are! If only they knew what you were really like, they would never want you to preach to them again.' I would feel physically sick and utterly worthless. The problem was that I knew my own heart and could not argue with this assessment of my life.

I'd get through the day, but then on the Monday morning when I felt at my most vulnerable and spent, that sense of condemnation would return with a vengeance. I knew there was a gap between what I proclaimed and how I lived. Again, I would find myself falling into the dark dungeon of despair.

As I look back, I am convinced that some of the gloom was the exhaustion of service – like Elijah, we are often most vulnerable when we have been most busy (1 Kings 19). However, the trigger was the feelings of guilt that pressed in on me. It was the chasm between what I thought I should be and what I knew I really was.

It's the gospel, stupid!

When it became almost too much to bear, I went to see an older pastor. I cannot stress enough the importance of seeking out the support and wisdom of older church leaders who have been on the road longer than us. For me, this guy was a lifesaver.

It was a lovely autumnal morning when I opened my heart to him. The air was crisp, and the sky was a breathtakingly beautiful azure blue. We walked together around a lake near his home. He allowed me to talk. I told him of my constant battles and frequent defeats. I was still going strong when he suggested that we sit on a bench. He let me finish my protestations: 'Don't you see that I cannot continue in my ministry until I stop sinning – which I can't do – or until I find some way to live with the guilt? What am I missing? What's the secret?'

When I was spent, he simply smiled and asked me, 'Have you never heard of the gospel?'

Now this is a rather embarrassing question to be asked as a preacher. I'm an evangelical, which means that I'm a gospel person. I believe that the gospel should be defined biblically, experienced personally and communicated passionately. Indeed, I love to invite people to come into the experience of the overwhelming grace of God – to come to Jesus and to know that their sins are forgiven once and forever.

What I discovered that day was that you can know the gospel, study the gospel, love the gospel and even preach the gospel, but that you can fail to feel its force at work in your life.

There is no special doctrine for leaders, no secret truth only discovered when you have been on the road for a few years. There is only the gospel. But the gospel is enough.

The gospel is still enough

As I look back on that gauche young man who was so over-whelmed with his own sinfulness, I feel a bit embarrassed to be writing these things down. Except that over the course of the years, I have met people who struggle with the same inner turmoil. I have talked with church leaders who have felt the strain so deeply that they have dropped out of ministry altogether. Others persevere, but constantly feel inadequate and condemned.

On the one hand, we should strive to overcome sin every day. As Christians, we are meant to be victors, not victims, to soar and not to sink, to overcome and not to be overwhelmed. We can, through God's grace, grow in our likeness to Christ and in real genuine holiness (see chapters 6 and 7).

On the other hand, sinless perfection is not a possibility this side of heaven. We must ask forgiveness for our sins every single day (Matthew 6:12). If we say we have no sin, we deceive ourselves (1 John 1:8 – 2:1). There will always be a gap between what we want to be and what we actually are. This is true of all followers of Jesus Christ. And we have to learn to live with the gap.

Maturity seasons us and helps us to cope. But it should also make us even more sensitive to sin and give us a deeper appreciation of the gloriously liberating power of the gospel.

The fall of a great man

My friend did more than remind me that I had forgotten the gospel. He told me to go home and meditate on Psalm 32.

Psalm 32 is one of the 'penitential psalms', and it describes the lessons that David learned in his own battle with failure. The context is almost certainly David's sin with Bathsheba. Now my situation was very different – I had not been unfaithful to my wife or fallen into sexual sin. However, much of what David had learned as his conscience was battered with the enormity of his transgression was applicable to my own battle with sin too and to my sense of personal unworthiness.

Second Samuel chapter 11 recounts David's fall. Instead of leading his army to war, he is relaxing at home. One evening he spies a young woman who is stunningly beautiful and particularly vulnerable (11:1–2). You cannot avoid the first look, but you don't have to indulge the second. And David goes much further than a second look. He makes inquiries, discovers her vulnerability, calls her into his home, sleeps with her and gets her pregnant (11:3–5).

Soon David discovers that once the genie is out of the bottle, you cannot put it back. He recalls Uriah, Bathsheba's husband, from the front and sets up a romantic rendezvous between husband and wife. Uriah refuses to play ball – does he suspect? (11:6–13). So then David takes the despicable step of arranging for Uriah's assassination (11:14–25). The man after God's own heart has become a cold and calculating murderer. Bathsheba is given a short time to grieve, and then David takes her as his wife and she bears him a son. David has got away with his sin – it seems that no-one suspects apart from the few people in the know. What is more, he has an attractive new wife and a brand new son.

However, the chapter ends on an ominous note: 'But the thing David had done displeased the LORD' (11:27).

For a considerable time the deception goes on, but eventually Nathan the prophet traps David into recognizing the depths of his sin (2 Samuel 12:1–7). David is forgiven, but God refuses to remove the consequences of his sin (12:8–14). The sword will never depart from his house (12:10). His baby son dies (12:15–23). David's sins of sexual incontinence, cunning deception and vicious violence are repeated by two of his grown-up sons (2 Samuel 13). His sin casts a malignant shadow over the rest of David's life, causing great sorrow and heartbreak even to the end (2 Samuel 14 – 1 Kings 2). There is a high cost to low living.

Lessons from failure

There are many lessons that leaders should learn from this story.

We are reminded of the particular dangers of middle age. This is good campaigning weather for the devil. Leaders with an exemplary record have often fallen in unexpected ways at this stage in their pilgrimage. Sexual temptation is an occupational hazard. Anyone can fall – yes, anyone!

David's tragic fall also shows us that forgiveness does not wipe out the consequences. Things would never be the same again for David. His reputation was shot to pieces, his kingdom was severely damaged and his family life was injured beyond repair. There are sins that we can commit which mean that we are disqualified from leadership for a considerable time, if not forever.

In addition, we learn that we should never turn any human leader into an idol. Yes, we can draw lessons from the leadership style of a variety of Bible characters. And there is nothing wrong with this, as long as we remember that the best of people are only people at their best. Part of the purpose of the David story must be to help us to recognize that we cannot idealize any 'son of Adam' – only Jesus, 'great David's greater Son', is worthy of unqualified adulation, honour and esteem. He is the true Shepherd of his people, the only leader we can follow with unreserved confidence.

A dreadful description

However, the overwhelming lesson is the amazing grace of God. It is difficult to grasp the magnitude of David's abuse of power or to plumb the depths of his contempt for God. And yet he experiences the amazing grace of God.

That is the theme of Psalm 32. God deals with our sin in a conclusive way and he does not want us to remember what he has chosen to forget.

The psalm begins with two beatitudes (32:1–2). The words may be translated: 'O how happy is the man'. It is an expression of blissful joy, delighted gladness and boundless happiness. We have been set free from every taint and blemish of guilt.

David does not play down the enormity of his sin, but uses three words to describe it:

'*Transgression*' is a positive word. It means to depart from God, to act deliberately and defiantly in rebellion against his will. It is to know God's laws and yet consciously, purposely and deliberately to break them.

'*Sin*' is a negative word, meaning to miss the mark and fall short. We were created to glorify God by loving him with all our heart and strength, and to find our greatest enjoyment in him. We have all fallen far short of this goal, despising his glory and delighting in anything other than God.

> *Sin is no small thing, because there is no small God to sin against.*

'*Iniquity*' (sin) means to be twisted or perverted, to be distorted or crooked. It reminds us that sin is a strange, crooked and irrational thing. We sin because we have an inbuilt bias towards bad. We are twisted and crooked. Sin leads to self-deception and spiritual blindness (32:2).

Sin is no small thing, because there is no small God to sin against. John Bunyan described it as 'a dare of God's justice, a rape of his mercy, a jeer at his patience, a slight of his power, a contempt of his love and a fist in his face'.[1]

We are right to be troubled about sin.

A glorious affirmation

But now David balances this against the magnitude of God's forgiveness. Again he uses three descriptions:

Our transgressions are 'forgiven'. The idea is of lifting up or lifting off and carrying away. The stain of our sin, which seemed to be so indelible, is lifted out and removed and never seen again. We are reminded of the annual Day of Atonement and the release of the scapegoat. One goat was sacrificed as a substitute for the sins of the nation, showing that without the shedding of blood there is no forgiveness of sin. The other goat, the scapegoat, was driven away into the wilderness, symbolically carrying away the people's sins, never to be seen again (Leviticus 16:20–22).

Our sins have been 'covered'. This word suggests blotting out or hiding from view. It means to cover over and conceal. God paints over the ugly graffiti of sin so that it is never seen again.

God 'does not count our sins (iniquities) against us'. He does not reckon them or keep an account of them. My dad worked in a grocer's shop in the 1950s. People really did buy goods 'on the slate'. At the back of the shop there was a big blackboard which recorded the customer's debts for the entire world to see. When the debt was finally settled, Dad would literally wipe the slate clean. There was no abiding record, just a residue of chalk dust. When God wipes out our sins, there is not even any chalk dust to show what we did.

Forgiveness is what defines me. We often fixate on the size of our church or the passion of our preaching or the depth of our theological knowledge or the zeal of our evangelism. However, these things cannot be allowed to define us. Who am I? I am a sinner who has come to experience the peerless grace of God and the stunning magnanimity of his forgiveness. Jesus, my scapegoat, has carried away my sin, for it never to be seen again. My heavenly Father has blotted out any memory of sin and made my slate clean.

A personal application

In the central section of this psalm David shares the lessons he has learned from this painful experience. His advice is very simple and straightforward: do what I did – but do it quicker! We all sin and fail. Don't waste time trying to hide it or justify it or ignore it or even wallow in it. Come to the fountain of God's grace and be cleansed instantly. Don't be silent; don't be slow; don't be stubborn.

His application consists of three directions:

Submit to God's discipline (32:3–5). For a considerable time David hid his sin and kept silent (32:3–4). On the outside, it may have looked like business as usual – the kingdom didn't fall apart, and no-one suspected anything. But that was only half of the story. On the inside, David was cracking up. His body was wasting away and his energy was sapped. He came to see that this was because God's hand was bearing down heavily on him. He was experiencing God's fatherly discipline. It was a severe mercy – God causing his pain so that in desperation he would come to repentance. In the words of C. S. Lewis, suffering 'removes the veil and it plants the flag of truth within the fortress of a rebel soul'.[2]

When he had come to the end of himself, David fled to God for mercy (32:5). Confession leads to forgiveness (1 John 1:9). Don't resist God's discipline or resent his intervention. Don't keep silent – you know it makes sense.

Trust in God's protection (3:6–8). In the face of overwhelming waters, we should seek God while he may be found. Life is fragile. Why delay? God offers protection and security to those who trust in him. This is the promise of Old Testament faith (Exodus 14:13–14; Jeremiah 17:5–8) and the invitation of Jesus (John 10:5–8[3]). God never intended us to bear the intolerable burden of guilt on our own shoulders. Listen to Charles Wesley:

> Jesus, Lover of my soul,
> Let me to Thy bosom fly,
> While the nearer waters roll,
> While the tempest still is high.

Hide me, O my Saviour, hide,
Till the storm of life is past;
Safe into the haven guide;
Oh, receive my soul at last.[4]

Make haste – don't be slow.

Listen to God's voice (32:9–11). God now speaks, and what a magnificent promise he gives. He will direct our lives and watch over the steps we take. This is no absentee landlord, but an ever-present, kind and faithful Father. But there is a condition. We must not rebel against his Word like a senseless animal which needs to be curbed and restricted. Don't fight God – you can't win! Don't be stubborn.

So the sum total of David's advice is that rather than wallowing in guilt and condemnation, we should quickly flee to the one place where we can find relief and help. Don't be silent; don't be slow; don't be stubborn.

A compelling invitation

The psalm ends with a summons to praise (32:11). Grace demands a response, and the most reasonable response is praise.

Have you noticed that when someone becomes a Christian, they become a singer? And this is not surprising. Music is powerful, and poetry is evocative. We celebrate key moments of our lives in song – they express the emotions that we are feeling. No wonder the book of Psalms is the longest book in the Bible. When we have grasped the splendour of forgiveness, we too will want to sing about it. As we sing, so we live.

And this was the second piece of advice that my wise pastor friend gave me. It ran something like this:

'Whenever you think about your sin and it becomes too heavy to bear, remember that it is forgiven sin. Instead of lamenting over it, praise God for forgiving it. Thank God that he chose to save you even though he knew you would let him down so often. Rejoice that he has promised never to finally forsake you. Remember what it cost him to forgive you – the death of his own Son. Turn your lamentation into jubilation and see what happens.'

I tried it – and it worked! I not only preached the gospel to my own heart, but I sang it.

And there is so much to sing about.

Sometimes we forget how great it is to be a Christian. The gospel covers our past, present and future. We have been justified: God the righteous Judge has declared that we are righteous in his sight. We do not need to fear the judgment of the last day, because God has already passed his verdict and will never change his mind.

We are being sanctified. The Holy Spirit is making us holy. The process may be slow, and there may be many times when we feel disappointed at our own sinfulness and stubborn resistance to his gentle yet persistent prompting. But he will not give up.

We will be glorified. One day the process of salvation will be completed, and in sinless bodies free from change and decay we will see God. Never again will we suffer. Never again will we sin. Never again will our lives be haunted by doubts or fears or anxieties.

The grace of God has made us children of God and brothers and sisters of Christ and citizens of the kingdom of God. In him, the poor are made rich and the weak are made strong. As Christians, we look forward to a glorious inheritance that will never perish nor spoil, never fade nor disappoint. It is reserved in heaven for us, and we are kept by the power of God through faith until the day when we finally receive it. There is now no condemnation for those who are in Christ Jesus. God works all things for our good, and even the darkest providences have an ultimate purpose. We are more than conquerors through him who loved us, and we know that nothing will ever separate us from his love. Nothing.

When we look back, there is no record of sin. When we look down, there is no hell to fear. When we look in, we find the peace of God which passes all understanding controlling our hearts and minds. When we look round, we see that God is working all things for our good. When we look forward, we see that Christ is coming to take us home – heaven dawns for us like a glorious and long-expected new day. We are saved and sealed and satisfied and secure.

It's great to be a Christian! Is it any wonder that we sing?

The cost of our forgiveness

But we haven't yet exhausted the depths of our subject. We cannot fully appreciate the glory of our forgiveness until we have begun to measure the immensity of God's gift to us in Christ. The most amazing thing about amazing grace is the cross of Jesus Christ.

John Duncan (1796–1870) was a Free Church of Scotland minister, a missionary to the Jews in Hungary and Professor of Hebrew and Oriental Languages at New College, Edinburgh. His grasp of the Hebrew language was so masterful and his love for Jewish people so deep that his students nicknamed him 'Rabbi Duncan'.

The most amazing thing about amazing grace is the cross of Jesus Christ.

On one occasion he was lecturing on the Hebrew text of Isaiah 53. For those unfamiliar with it, this is a messianic passage pointing forward to Christ's substitutionary death for sinners. Duncan came to verse 6:

> We all, like sheep, have gone astray,
>   each of us has turned to our own way;

and the L<small>ORD</small> has laid on him
the iniquity of us all.

In the middle of his exposition he was overcome with the
magnitude of it. So much so that for a full two minutes he could
not speak. Finally gaining some control over his emotions
and with tears running down his cheeks, he broke the silence:
'Gentlemen, gentlemen, it was damnation and he took it lovingly
. . . He took it for us!'[5]

Films like *The Passion of the Christ* concentrate on the physical
sufferings of Jesus which were truly dreadful. Crucifixion was
designed to be the ultimate deterrent, and it involved excruciating pain and appalling shame.

But for Jesus, that was not the most horrific thing about
the cross. In the three hours of darkness that descended on the
mount of crucifixion, God placed the guilt of all our sins on his
innocent Son and then treated him as if he was responsible for
all of them. The punishment deserved by David's adultery and
Peter's denials and Paul's persecutions and all the sins of a
numberless crowd of fallen people were all executed on Jesus.
He entered into the darkness of condemnation and the pains
of hell during those hours. It was damnation, and he took it –
for us.

Throughout his lifetime Jesus walked under the conscious
smile of his Father's love. The first and last words recorded
during his earthly life refer to God as his Father (Luke 2:49;
23:46). It was his usual way of addressing God – indeed, he uses
the title over 150 times in the Gospels. Even as he is being
crucified, he prays, 'Father, forgive' (Luke 23:34). But out of
the darkness of damnation comes the wringing lament: 'My
God, my God, why have you forsaken me?' (Matthew 27:45–46;
Psalm 22:1). 'God made him who had no sin to be sin for us,
so that in him we might become the righteousness of God'
(2 Corinthians 5:21).

What difference should this make to our leadership?

It should make us love the Father for giving up his Son for us and make us love Jesus for dying in our place. We should hate sin and try, with God's power, to put it to death. If the cross is God's answer to sin, then it shows us the enormity of the offence. When Satan tempts us to despair over the guilt of our sins, we need to return to the cross and recognize that such an amazing sacrifice is sufficient to deal with all sins, past, present and future. We should rejoice at the certainty and security of our salvation. Purchased at such measureless cost, it can never be lost.

Abiding convictions

When I preach now, it is with two deep and abiding convictions.

Firstly, I can only stand in front of others because I stand in the grace of God. I am a forgiven sinner. I continue to be a sinner in need of daily forgiveness. It's not a bad thing to remind people of this.

Secondly, every Christian sitting in front of me is struggling with the same problem; we are all in the same boat. If we have any self-knowledge at all, we feel that we are hypocrites who are not living up to our best aspirations. And as a 'wounded physician', I can bring the medicine of God's grace into broken lives.

Questions

1. Why are leaders particularly vulnerable to a sense of failure and condemnation?
2. When do you find yourself most vulnerable in this area? How do we recognize fatigue, and what should we do about it?

3. 'What I discovered that day was that you can know the gospel, study the gospel, love the gospel and even preach the gospel, but that you can fail to feel its force at work in your life.' What can we do to ensure that we feel the force of the gospel at work in our lives?

4. How does understanding the nature of Christ's work on the cross help us to combat condemnation? What other Christian truths can help us when we feel condemned?

5. Read the penitential psalms (Psalms 6; 32; 51; 102; 130; 143). What health-giving truths can you find here?

11. Control your diary

Confession is supposed to be good for the soul.

When our children were small, we went to the seaside one year for a break. I left my wife resting on the beach while I took our four kids to a play park. The older three ran off to do their own thing, so I was left looking after our two-year-old. We played on the swings and shot down the slide. We chuckled at our distorted reflections in the house of mirrors. We rode the carousel together.

And then we discovered the ball pool.

My daughter had never experienced such a phenomenon before and was thrilled to be able to thrash about in perfectly safe and secure surroundings. For me, it was a great boon. I had brought a book with me – I never go anywhere without a book. So, while she continued to explore her environment, I sat at the side and watched her over the top of my book.

Everything went well for a while, but then I got distracted – I had reached a particularly engaging passage. I forgot my daughter and did not look up for several minutes. When I did so, she was nowhere to be seen.

Of course I panicked. I was sitting by the entrance – there was no way that she could have left. But where was she? I called her name. No answer. I looked about frantically – no sign of her. Then, just as I was about to seek help, my eye was drawn to a small pink fist sticking up above the balls. She had sunk down into the amorphous slew of balls and was unable to dig her way out as hundreds of multicoloured spheres closed over her head.

Once I had pulled her out, she was fine, and I was careful to keep the story under wraps.

Please don't tell my wife.

Buried in business

Why do I tell this story?

Because, although I have never experienced the terror of being buried in a ball pool, there have been several times in my ministry when I have been overwhelmed by the demands of leadership. This is usually the result of allowing other people to dictate my agenda, and failing to prioritize.

For a while a personal assistant kept my diary for me. It was during the time when I was engaged in a number of activities beyond my church. I was worried about being swamped, so I asked a small accountability group to set some guidelines, and then one of the group was appointed to administer the guidelines and control the number of engagements I took on. The arrangement worked very well.

But when I took over my own diary again, I failed to exercise the same discipline and found that I was swamped. It took a couple of years to regain equilibrium. The problem was a failure to plan. I learned that I needed to use my diary as a spiritual tool.

Planning is not 'unspiritual'. Paul frequently operated according to clear plans. He could change them if circumstances demanded, or if God directed otherwise. But he knew what he wanted to do and what was necessary to see it achieved.

Those who fail to plan, plan to fail. If you cannot do it yourself, get someone to help you. In my experience, it is a lack of planning which causes the greatest anxiety.

Time is one of the most valuable gifts that God has given us.

Bible guidelines

The Bible says a lot about time management. We all need to develop a theology of time. It would be impossible to be exhaustive, but here are four principles to think, pray and work through.

Time is a gift from God – don't take it for granted

Like every good gift we enjoy, time is a gift from the hand of a Father who loves to bless us with good things (James 1:17). It is easy to take it for granted and think that it is endless. However, Moses tells us to 'number our days, that we may gain a heart of wisdom' (Psalm 90:12). Notice that he does not mention years or even weeks. Time comes to us in little packets that we call 'days'. The only packet we are promised is the one we are enjoying at this moment. Our times are in God's hands (Psalm 31:14–15). He has determined exactly how long we will live (Psalm 139:16). As I write this page, I have lived for 21,257 days. This is my 21,257th birthday! How many days do I have left? Only God knows!

This is quite sobering. It's also very realistic. We should never take tomorrow for granted. Life is a mist that appears for a little while and then it is gone. So we should live our lives in humble gratitude for the gift of today (James 4:13–17).

Time is a valuable resource – spend it wisely

God expects us to be careful about the way we use our time. If it is as limited as the Bible teaches, then the wise person will make the most of every opportunity. When I was a teenager, our youth leader and his wife had a poster on the wall next to where they fed their messy three-year-old. It portrayed a toddler sitting in a high chair. He had taken a bowl of very gooey spaghetti and placed it upside down on his head like a sticky crown. The goo was running everywhere. Underneath was the text: 'This is the day that the Lord has made, I *will* be glad and rejoice in it' (see Psalm 118:24)! That represents the determination of faith! Whatever happens, I will make the most of the next twenty-four hours, and even in times of trial I will rejoice in God.

In Ephesians 5:16 Paul talks about 'making the most of every opportunity' God gives us. The word he uses is related to the Greek word *agora*. The *agora* was the marketplace. When we visit a market, we make a number of choices. What shall I buy? How much will I spend? What can I afford? As we face each day, we are called to make choices and not waste the limited resource of time. Each day brings new opportunities which may never be repeated. So don't waste what you have. Someone once asked John Wesley what he would do if he realized that today was his last day on earth. He showed them a very full diary. Then he said, 'I would do everything written here. At the end of the day I would go to sleep knowing that I had done all I could to please God. I would close my eyes, and wake to glory.'[1] In other words, every day was planned as if it were his last. Good plan!

Time is a precious asset – invest it carefully

As we shall see below, we need time to rest and play as well as to work and labour. However, we need to remember that we only have one life to live for God and only limited time in which to glorify him. That is why the needs of God's kingdom should take priority. Jesus commanded us, 'But seek first his kingdom and his righteousness, and all these things will be given to you as well' (Matthew 6:33).

As leaders, we have the amazing privilege of investing in the lives of men and women. Most leadership will involve tasks that we think are pretty mundane. But if they contribute to the building of God's kingdom, then they have great value. We need to make choices between legitimate alternatives. Kingdom thinking can enable us to do this successfully.

Time is a limited commodity – don't squander it
The Bible contains a catalogue of warnings about laziness (Proverbs 10:4; 12:24, 27; 13:4, to name just a few). Some leaders are lazy and need to buck up their ideas. But in my experience, this is relatively rare. The greater danger is that we fill our lives with the things we enjoy doing in order to avoid the things we find more demanding and less attractive. John Ortberg describes it as the failure to do what we should do when it needs to be done, 'like the Kamikaze pilot who flew seventeen missions'.[2] Workaholics can unconsciously be guilty of this. They allow the daily demands to push aside challenging tasks that they would prefer to ignore. Ortberg lists some of the telltale signs: 'an odd combination of hurry and wastefulness. I rush in the morning, telling my wife I have no time for breakfast, no time to see the kids off to school; too much to do. Later in the morning, I read the sports section or make an unnecessary phone call.' Don't waste your time.

Establishing priorities

There is a demonstration that I have heard about but have never seen performed.

The presenter shows his audience a large glass jar with a funnel at the top. He begins to put large rocks into this jar until no more will fit.

Is the jar full? The answer seems obvious, and the audience agrees that the jar has reached its capacity.

From under the table he brings a box containing tiny pebbles. When he pours these into the neck of the glass jar, they fill the remaining spaces around the rocks quite comfortably.

The audience smiles at the deception, but agrees for a second time that the jar really is full now!

At which point our presenter pulls out a bag of sand. The tiny grains scurry down the neck of the jar and find a place surrounding the pebbles.

What next? By now the audience will not be tricked again – they don't know how anything else can be placed into the jam-packed jar, but they are certain that it can.

And of course they are right. The man takes a bottle of water. It fills the tiny spaces surrounding the grains of sand. The jar is finally full to capacity.

But what's the point of this?

I think there are two things that are helpful for our purpose in this chapter: a warning and an illustration.

The warning first. Often our lives resemble the jar at the end of the exercise. We have filled it to its absolute capacity. There is room for nothing else. This may seem like a good thing, but I'm not so sure. If our life is so crowded that there is room for nothing else, we may find ourselves living at the ragged edge. We may continue for a while, but in the end the jar will shatter.

What about the illustration? Surely the main point of the demonstration is to encourage us to think carefully about priorities. To put it in another way, make sure that you put the rocks in first. Decide on the non-negotiables and stick to them. You may fill the gaps with other things, but if you fail to get your priorities right, you will crash and burn.

Failure to prioritize

If God puts us in a situation where we find ourselves stretched to the limit, then we will discover that his grace is sufficient. But most of the time the pressures are self-imposed and a result of foolish overcommitment. It is not God's desire that we should overcommit. We do it because we have forgotten how to say 'no'.

We cannot allow others to set our agenda for us. There is always enough time for the things that God wants us to do.

Why do we allow this to happen?

There are a variety of reasons why we fail to prioritize. Work through the following list. Which ones apply to you?

- We are driven by a desire to please people – we are afraid to say 'no'.
- We justify ourselves by our work rate – the more we do, the more we feel God's smile on us. If we lead a church, we are aware of the common misconception that ministers are six days invisible and one day incomprehensible. Not me!
- We feel threatened by others – how can I hold on to my ministry, position or office? By making myself indispensable!
- We are too lazy to plan – it is easier to say 'yes'.
- We don't like delegating because it is easier to do it ourselves than to trust someone else.
- We have never seriously considered the priorities that should shape us.

What are the results of this overcommitment?

Failure to prioritize can have devastating results. Read through this list and see if you can recognize any similar patterns in your own life:

- We are dragged into a vortex of activity which leaves no room for reflection.
- Pebbles become rocks, and rocks become pebbles. We neglect the cultivation of our souls because we have no time for it.
- We find ourselves becoming indispensable. This feeds our pride, but damages the church.

- Our self-image depends on our busyness. We find ourselves on a treadmill in which the harder we work, the guiltier we become.
- Our wife and children suffer. They cannot compete with the demands of ministry – how could they?
- We become disillusioned and depressed, and if we do nothing about it, we rapidly approach burn-out.
- We find ourselves unable to resist temptations. Many Christian leaders fall into unprecedented sin when they are exhausted.

Ministry priorities

What are the core priorities of gospel ministry?

⇨ Matthew 28:18–20 – Make disciples
⇨ Acts 6:2, 4 – Prayer and the Word
⇨ 2 Timothy 1:14 – Guard the gospel
⇨ 2 Timothy 2:2 – Pass on the gospel
⇨ 2 Timothy 3:14–16 – Continue in the gospel
⇨ 2 Timothy 4:1–5 – Preach the gospel
⇨ Ephesians 4:11–12 – Train God's people
⇨ John 21:15–17 – Feed the flock

Keep your focus!

Select your rocks very carefully

So how do we determine our priorities?

To some extent the order of our priorities will differ from person to person, but here are ten clear biblical guidelines to help us. Take time to work through them carefully and prayerfully.

1. Our walk with God

This is invisible and therefore often the first priority to go. We need to work hard to have adequate time for prayer and reflection. Speaking personally, I try to devote the first hour of the day to reading the Bible and praying. I couldn't always do this when my children were small. And there are still times when for legitimate reasons the time is cut short. It is important not to allow our time with God to become a means of self-justification. If it is missed, this does not mean that the day will be a disaster. Sometimes you will also need to mark off special time in the diary in order to recharge your batteries. I occasionally feel the need to block out an afternoon or even a whole day. In the diary this appears as 'TWG' – 'Time with God'. It is a priority because it is in the diary. And I can legitimately tell those who are demanding my time that I already have an appointment. If I am to serve others effectively, I will need to maintain this most intimate of relationships. Prayer is hard work. It has been described as the 'sweat of the soul'. It demands effort and energy. We need to give it the quality time required to enable it to flourish.

2. The demands of marriage and family

As argued in chapter 8, our entire ministry comes out of the context of the home. We need to create times that are protected from the demands of ministry, and our spouse and offspring should know that they are a priority. If we have made a commitment, we must not let them down – we need to keep our word. If we miss a date with our wife or a breakfast with our son or a football match with our daughter because another ministry demand has stolen our attention, we will come to regret it later. And it is more than just time that is needed – it is quality time.

I have often taken Mondays off. This suits my make-up – I like to rest after a busy Sunday, and then on Tuesday morning begin to climb the hill for the next Sunday's ministry. This is great in theory, but what it means is that often my wife gets the least productive and creative time of the whole week. Sometimes the lights are on but there's no-one at home. What does this communicate to my wife? That ministry is more important than marriage. This, as we saw earlier, should not be so.

3. The demands of ministry

The work of ministry is demanding. If we are ministers or pastors, it is a job that is never finished. We are called to present people 'fully mature' in Christ (Colossians 1:28). This will never be completed until they get to heaven. So we can never sign off on anyone. Our lives are entwined with those of people we love. Their pains will be our pains, and their joys will be our joys. And then every week we have to preach a new message which is faithful and relevant and deeply moving. On top of this, there are a whole series of regular demands as well as unforeseen emergencies. We will never survive unless we learn to prioritize and to delegate.

4. The need to rest

God rested after he had created the world, thereby setting an example that we need to follow. We might call this the 'Sabbath principle'. I don't know whether there will be sleep in heaven, but in a fallen world it is certainly essential for continued health. Occasionally we may need to sacrifice our sleep for necessary reasons. However, we cannot make this a regular practice. Know yourself. How much sleep do you need in order to function? What are the signs of fatigue that warn you of danger? In what other ways do you rest?

5. The need to recreate

We are made in the image of a God who creates with infinite variety and beauty. Creativity is built into our DNA. For some people it is obvious – their creative gifts are evident. But all of us need to find the time and energy to do things that help us to relax and unwind the taut twine of our lives. We need regular stress-busters. For me, it is reading military history, walking along the Birmingham canal to Gas Street Basin, playing with my granddaughters, enjoying a romantic meal with my wife or cheering on West Bromwich Albion (although supporting the 'Baggies' is often a source of stress rather than a stress-buster). It will be different for you, but I would suggest that this is a priority which is necessary for your mental health and well-being.

6. The need to plan
One of the reasons why we fail to prioritize is that we fail to plan. Planning seems so unspiritual. Isn't it dictating to God? Isn't it expecting God to fit in with our plans? It can be – but not necessarily. When we prayerfully plan our diary, we are able to establish our priorities and remove those pressures that arise when we don't give ourselves the necessary time to complete a task. We can identify periods of particularly busy activity and surround them with quieter, less demanding times. Lack of planning leads to anxiety as we lurch from one crisis to another. If you cannot plan, get someone to help you.

7. The need to invest in people
In chapter 9 we saw the importance of relationships. You may lead a group of Sunday school teachers or home-group leaders or another ministry team. And you will need to find time to invest in them. You may even have identified individuals who are potential leaders for the future. One of your most productive uses of time will be to spend it with these next-generation leaders. However, you will also need friends, and friendship demands time. With whom do you work, rest and play? Who makes you smile?

8. The need to make friends with non-Christians
It is not only Christians in whom we need to invest the necessary time for lasting relationships, but non-Christians. Jesus was the

166 | STAYING FRESH

friend of sinners. He spoke with them, created time to be with them and even ate with them. In his culture that was a radical thing to do. He flouted the accepted norms of the day in order to befriend them and create opportunities to bring them the good news. And we are called to follow in his footsteps. Think for a moment. How many non-Christians belong to your friendship circle? Churches can become quite expert at putting on well-run evangelistic events, but the problem is that very few non-Christians come to them. Why? Because we do not have the kind of relationships that will enable us to invite them to the event in the first place. Why should they be interested in the things we do if we are not interested in their lives? And it is not just for the sake of gospel opportunities that we are to build such friendships. We will want to share what is most precious to us obviously, but if they reject our message, do we reject them? Of course not!

9. The demands of employment

Ministry may not be your full-time employment. Or if you are leading a church, circumstances may demand that you supplement your income by working outside it. The first thing to recognize is that whatever calling we have, we should see it as coming from God, and the sphere in which we are called to serve him. It is not merely the sphere in which we earn enough money to fund our real work of Christian ministry. The Bible knows no secular/sacred distinction. Paul says, 'Whatever you do, work at it with all your heart, as working for the Lord, not for human masters' (Colossians 3:23). So work is a priority – for many of us the most pressing and time-consuming priority of our lives. We should not feel guilty about promotion, but at the same time we need to avoid the temptation to allow our career to become an idol that consumes our energies and passions. It may be difficult, but somehow we need to work out ways to prevent our daily employment from controlling our lives and strangling every other priority.

10. *The need to stretch our minds*

The Christian has a mind and should be grateful for it. The process of growing in the Christian life is accompanied by the renewal of our minds (Romans 12:1–2). We are encouraged to love God with our minds (Matthew 22:37–38) and to prepare them for action (1 Peter 1:13). This means that we should give our minds the opportunity to be stretched. We should be reading books that challenge us. It's good for us to wrestle with big doctrines. We need to create time to make use of all the facilities of a multimedia world to push out the limits of our understanding. Physical exercise and health are important – so too is the health of the mind.

All this is pretty demanding. Indeed, just looking at the above list can be exhausting! Sometimes we feel like shutting up shop and running away. But the Bible does not give me this option. I am to work hard and treat time as a valuable God-given commodity that must not be wasted.

But how do we do this without burning out? We will explore that question in the next chapter.

Questions

1. Consider the four principles in the section 'Bible guidelines'. What are the practical implications of each principle as far as your life and service are concerned?
2. Look at the list of 'Ministry priorities'. How should they affect the emphasis of the particular ministry that you are involved in?
3. 'There is always time for the things that God wants us to do.' How do we determine what these things are?
4. Why do we fail to plan? What are the results of this failure?

5. Review the list of ten priorities above. Are there any others that you would want to add? Which do you find most difficult? Why? What could you do about it?

12. Remember you are human

I can still remember my ordination into Christian ministry.

It was a very cold January day. The service lasted for two hours. My wife and I made promises. These were followed by promises from the church. It felt like getting married again.

In those days there were two sermons: an address to the church and an address to the pastor. The sermon to the church was a call to prayer from a seasoned pastor named Will Parsons. He said that the best thing you can do for your pastor is to pray for him. Pray for his health – physical and spiritual. Pray for his family. Pray for his ministry. It was great stuff, and I remember it all very clearly, even though it was over thirty years ago. I didn't know it at the time, but his advice was excellent, and through the trials that my wife and I faced in the years that lay ahead, the loving prayer and support of our fellow Christians was one of the reasons why we survived.[1]

The second sermon was addressed directly to me. My own pastor Les Coley delivered it. I had come to faith under his ministry, and his preaching had been the single biggest cause of my own spiritual growth. Les spoke from Paul's words to the Ephesian elders as recorded in Acts 20:13–35. This is a

wide-ranging passage which deals with motivation and method
and manner of ministry. As he reached his climax, Les took off
his spectacles, leaned across the pulpit and drew my attention to
verse 24:

> However, I consider my life worth nothing to me; my only aim is
> to finish the race and complete the task the Lord Jesus has given
> me – the task of testifying to the good news of God's grace.

'Remember Paul's example,' Les said. 'God gave him a race to
run and a task to fulfil. For Paul it was the thing that controlled
his life. It was more important than life and death to him. Today
God has given you that task. Spend your life doing it.'

I can still remember the tingle that ran down my spine.

If there is one verse that has shaped my approach to ministry
more than any other, it is that one. It has often acted as both a
challenge and an encouragement. It has reminded me of priorities and challenged my laziness or cowardice. It has been an
antidote to timidity and faintheartedness. It has reminded me of
my high calling and ultimate accountability to God.

Heed the challenge

In Acts 20:24 Paul is talking about the life-and-death challenge
of Christian leadership. He is confronting our coolness and
cowardice: 'Don't be soft. Don't be self-indulgent. Spend yourself
in the service of the one who spent himself to save you.'

People are still dying for the sake of the gospel. It is a high
statistical probability that even as you are reading this book,
somewhere in the world someone has laid down their life for
their faith in Christ. In the West we know little about this level
of sacrifice. So often we lament the 'cost of ministry', but know
little of what it really means.

We would do well to heed Paul's words.

We reflected on this in chapter 4. As Christians, we follow a crucified Saviour. As leaders, we are called to lay down our lives for the people we serve. If we are unwilling to make sacrifices, we had better do something else, for we have failed to understand the ground rules. In our culture we may not be called to lay down our lives for Christ, but we are called to die to our own desires and ambitions and comforts.

Remember C. S. Lewis's words:

> To love at all is to be vulnerable. Love anything and your heart will be wrung and possibly broken. If you want to make sure of keeping it intact, you must give it to no one, not even an animal. Wrap it carefully round with hobbies and little luxuries; avoid all entanglements. Lock it up safe in the casket or coffin of your selfishness. But in that casket, safe, dark, motionless, airless, it will change. It will not be broken; it will become unbreakable, impenetrable, irredeemable. To love is to be vulnerable.[2]

Love for Christ, for his people and for a lost world makes us vulnerable. It is also the ruling passion that drives us forward and tinctures our sacrifice with joy. Here is something worth spending your life on. Sometimes we need to abandon our carefully constructed safety zones and stretch ourselves in God's service.

When I have felt self-pity or discouragement, I have turned back to Paul's words in Acts 20:24. I thank God for the spur that it has been.

But just occasionally my misinterpretation or misapplication of Paul's words has been a stumbling block. This has sometimes led to an unwise overcommitment, which has resulted in exhaustion with all the dangers that that entails.

Strike a balance

I think that it was the Welsh Nonconformist minister Christmas

Evans who once declared, 'It is better to burn out than to rust out in the service of the Lord.'[3]

It's an attractive sentiment – but is it right?

To put it another way, what level of stress is acceptable in the lives of leaders?

Stress has been defined as that sense of stretch that we find when it seems that our challenges are greater than our perceived resources. It is not a bad thing in itself. Indeed, sometimes it is good to be stretched. If we were never stretched, we would never need to exercise faith. Stress pushes us beyond our safety zone and encourages us to trust God.

But it can easily become unhealthy and debilitating. We overcommit ourselves. We take on more than we can cope with. We lose our sense of perspective. As a result, we can become careless about things that we should protect. We don't rest as we should. We are too busy or too tired to pray. Our marriage suffers. We become moody and withdrawn. We may explode in unexpected and unjustifiable anger. Or we may internalize our anger and fall into a state of brooding bitterness. This may be followed by dejection – there is a close connection between anger and depression. It is always winter and never Christmas in our souls. We begin to feel resentment about the way God is treating us. Why is it so hard to be faithful? Why did God put so much on my shoulders? We forget that the situation is the result of our own overcommitment and lack of wisdom.

At such times we lose all our freshness and joy. Christian discipleship becomes a chore, and Christian service becomes an unbearable burden. What is the point of serving God?

In my experience, these are the most dangerous times in our lives. Our spiritual defences are more easily breached. We are in danger of committing sins that would be unthinkable on other occasions. This adds to the spiral. Once we have sinned, we feel even worse about ourselves. We are susceptible to even worse temptations – what is the point of fighting against sin when I am such a wretched failure? Depression turns to despair, and it is difficult to see any light in the darkness. How could God allow this to happen to me when I have been so faithful to him?

The root cause of this condition is not my commitment to Christ; it is my unwise failure to correctly marshal my resources. It is the result of overwork, behind which there is often a desire for self-justification. I work hard in order to justify my existence and somehow increase my worthiness before God. This is self-driven rather than grace-directed.

Here is my dilemma: I want to heed the challenge of Acts 20:24, but I don't want to fall into the familiar spiral. Is it possible to do both?

Commenting on the words of Christmas Evans, James Berkley made the following statement:

> I admire the bravado. It sounds dedicated, bold, and stirring. However, when I view the burnt-outs and the almost burnt-outs who lie by the ecclesiastical road, the glory fails to reach me. I see pain and waste and unfinished service. Is there not a third alternative to either burning out or rusting out? In Acts 20:24 Paul stated, 'I consider my life worth nothing to me, if only I may finish the race and complete the task the Lord Jesus has given me.' Herein lies the model I choose to follow. I want neither to burn out nor rust out. I want to finish out the race.[4]

I too want neither to burn out nor rust out. I want to finish the race. Here is wisdom. Berkley's interpretation of Paul's words strikes a helpful balance.

Know yourself

One of the most valuable lessons that I think I have learned in my years of Christian leadership is the importance of knowing ourselves. We are all different and respond in different ways to different circumstances. We have different stress points and can cope with different amounts of pressure. What will sink one person will cause another to soar.

I am very good in the morning. I usually get up between 5 and 6 am and am ready to face the day. I feel uncomfortable if I am still in bed after 6 – if it is after 7 then I must be ill. I'm not boasting here – it's just the way I am. It's actually the way I always have been, even as a student. But from around 4 pm I begin to wilt. Before my knees gave way, I used to go for a run, which seemed to reinvigorate me. These days I either go for a walk or have a power nap. Then I can face a rash of evening meetings, but I always try to finish by 10 pm. To sustain my health, I need to be in bed before 11 pm.

What happens if I try to stay up late or to break the routine in some way? I usually fail to catch up on sleep and find myself becoming irritable and listless. Over the years I have come to recognize that this is the way I work. Could I change it? Maybe, but I'm not sure what the reason would be.

Of course there have been times when the routine has had to change. When the children woke us in the middle of the night, when my wife needed nursing, when emergencies of ministry have intervened, I have had to change my timetable. But most of the time I have found that this routine is what optimizes my usefulness in ministry.

Other people are very different. I am a lark – up before the sun. Dr Martyn Lloyd-Jones, for many years the pastor of Westminster Chapel in central London, was an owl. He once entertained a visiting American preacher who insisted on getting him up early in the morning to discuss deep theological issues. Lloyd-Jones was quite grumpy about this, until that same evening he kept the man talking until late into the night. 'In the morning he almost killed me; in the evening I returned the favour!'[5]

We must be what we are. Self-knowledge is important. God does not expect you to be someone or something that you are not. God is the God of both creation and redemption. In creation he formed your temperament and gifts and capacities.

When you become a Christian, grace transforms you. But grace does not significantly alter your personality. It may refine it and iron out the kinks. But an extrovert does not become an introvert. A phlegmatic does not suddenly become choleric. A sanguine does not become melancholic. A lark does not become an owl.

Be yourself. That is how God made you and how he wants you to be. Of course this should never be used as an excuse for sin: 'I cannot help losing my temper because that's the way I'm made.' Grace deals with the sinful defects of our character, and the response to sin is always confession and repentance. But don't expect your personality to change. Being what God made you to be pleases your Creator and brings him most glory. He did not make a mistake when he made you what you are.

Lack of self-knowledge

If we fail to know ourselves, certain things will follow. (We touched on this earlier.)

- We will compare ourselves to others in an unhealthy way. Christian biographies will poleaxe us – why can't we be like these great people we are reading about?
- If we have a higher capacity for activity than others, this may lead to pride and a critical spirit. If our capacity is less, we will feel guilty and may become bitter towards those who seem able to achieve more.
- We will set ourselves unrealistic targets and beat ourselves up if we fail to reach them. We will push ourselves beyond our personal limits of endurance and find ourselves sinking in the cesspit of overwork.
- We will stop enjoying our leadership and find that it becomes an overwhelming burden.

- We will sometimes identify problems wrongly, thinking we have a spiritual problem when it is no such thing. Often the issues that we think are spiritual are actually physical or psychological.
- We will begin to doubt God's wisdom or love, or both. Why did God make me like this? Surely it's a mistake?

Remember you're a jar of clay

Beyond this personal knowledge, we need to have a realistic knowledge of ourselves as human beings. We are fearfully and wonderfully made. Alone of all God's creatures we have been made in his image. What a spectacle is humankind!

At the same time, we are fallen creatures in a fallen world. In some of the most perceptive words in the Bible, the apostle Paul contrasts the gospel with those called to preach it. The good news of salvation is phenomenally powerful. It is like the original creative Word of God, which brought light out of darkness:

> For what we preach is not ourselves, but Jesus Christ as Lord, and ourselves as your servants for Jesus' sake. For God, who said, 'Let light shine out of darkness,' made his light shine in our hearts to give us the light of the knowledge of God's glory displayed in the face of Christ.
> (2 Corinthians 4:5–6)

But how does Paul describe the person who carries this message?

> But we have this treasure in jars of clay to show that this all-surpassing power is from God and not from us.
> (4:7)

A jar of clay was the first-century equivalent of a plastic bag: frail, disposable and of little value. This description of what we are is both honest and humbling. We are 'frail children of dust and feeble as frail'.[6]

Never forget that you are human. Dr Arch D. Hart has observed that 'Most ministers don't burn out because they forget they are ministers. They burn out because they forget they are persons.'[7]

If we fail to cope with stress for a significant length of time, it can easily lead to depression or even burn-out. Recognizing the signs and acting accordingly is vital.

Remember, not every problem is a spiritual problem

One of the most important principles to remember is that not every problem is a spiritual problem.

Quite early on in my ministry I faced a demanding and confusing pastoral situation. Graham (not his real name), an older man, was struggling with depression. There were examples of depressive illness in the family – both his father and brother had been hospitalized because of it. Now Graham was manifesting similar symptoms. One day he was visiting a Christian bookshop when someone unhelpfully suggested that his depressive thoughts were the result of demonic possession. He needed to be exorcized, and they offered to do the service for him. What followed was so distressing that it drove Graham into a spiral of mental disintegration.

When his wife called me in, she was in despair and didn't know how to cope. Graham was behaving irrationally. He was convinced that an evil spirit was controlling him. He couldn't possibly be a Christian. I tried to reason from the Bible, but could get nowhere. He did not respond to spiritual medicine, and it slowly dawned on me that this was because he did not have a spiritual problem. He used spiritual words, but the problem was with the functioning of his brain. The history of mental illness in the family confirmed this diagnosis. Of course I could offer him encouragement and support, but in the end his real need was for medical help and back-up. Much of my time was spent seeking to encourage his wife and family, and helping them to make the distinction between mental/physical problems and spiritual ones. Eventually, and after medical treatment, Graham was able to respond to the support I was able to bring him from the Bible.

Most of the problems we face are difficult to unravel. Where do the physical, mental and spiritual interface? How do we distinguish between them?

The answer is often quite complicated, but there is one principle that I have found most helpful: spiritual problems respond to spiritual medicine; psychological problems respond to psychological medicine; physical problems respond to physical medicine.

We see this illustrated in the story of Elijah (1 Kings 19). Under extreme pressure, he faced a crisis of faith. It seemed as if his efforts to confront evil had completely failed:

> I have been very zealous for the LORD God Almighty. The Israelites have rejected your covenant, torn down your altars, and put your prophets to death with the sword. I am the only one left, and now they are trying to kill me too.
> (19:10)

I don't think this is self-pity – it is the cry of a man who is passionately committed to God's cause. The effects are so devastating that he despairs even of life, and asks to die (19:4).

God encourages his servant with a fresh vision of the invincibility of his purposes – the work of purging Israel of evil will certainly be accomplished (19:11–18). However, before the spiritual medicine is applied, God first deals with Elijah's physical condition. He gives him two very simple and yet vitally necessary gifts: sleep and sustenance (food and drink: 19:3–9). Until he is refreshed physically, he is not capable of processing

the theological truths which will lift him up and lead to several
more years of fruitful service.

Use sanctified common sense

What do we need if we are to survive? It's really a matter of
sanctified common sense. Consider the following questions:

- *Sleep:* Are you getting enough? Is your sleep refreshing?
  Do you wake up ready to face the day?
- *Rest:* Do you keep a weekly day for rest and refreshment?
  If you are in full-time ministry, do you take a day off to
  compensate for a busy Sunday?
- *Stress-busters:* What are the things that enable you to
  escape stress? It may be golf or cross-stitch or *Star Trek*
  – it's your call. What do you do to 'unstring your bow'?
  What things help you to forget pressure for a while? What
  makes you laugh?
- *Pit stops:* How often do you step outside the busyness
  of life and refuel? How often do you stop and smell the
  roses? When was the last time you had a really refreshing
  holiday?
- *Care for your body:* Do you think of your body as the
  temple of the Holy Spirit? What do you do to maximize
  your health? What exercise do you take? Are you
  overweight? When was your last medical MOT?
- *Care for your mind:* What do you do to maximize your
  mental health? Can you pick up the early-warning signs
  of oncoming depression? What do you do to prevent it?
  What do you do about anxiety, anger and self-pity?
- *Make friends:* How many friends do you have, and with
  whom you can really relax and be yourself?
- *Sex:* If you are married, how is your sex life? Do you
  create time to be romantic with your spouse?

- *Abandon the idolatry of achievement:* Do you feel that you are indispensable? Would your church collapse without you? Do you live for your ministry and the sense of achievement that it brings?
- *Combat perfectionism:* Are you a perfectionist? What are the dangers of perfectionism? How do you overcome it?
- *Avoid overwork:* What makes you want to be constantly busy? How do you avoid getting stretched beyond your ability to endure? Have you learned to say 'no'? Do you control your digital devices or do they control you?
- *Be realistic in your expectations:* How do you cope with disappointment and failure? What do you do when things don't work out as you had hoped?
- *Avoid a false asceticism:* Do you ever despise the good gifts that God has generously given you? Do you gladly receive them with thanksgiving? Do you enjoy good music? Good food? Do you know how to have fun?
- *Balance:* Would you describe your life as balanced? Do you care for your body, mind and soul? How?

Sensible sacrifice?

Christian biographies can inform, educate, challenge and inspire. They help us to see God at work and they feed our faith. But they can also be dangerous, as we saw earlier. These great men and women were often one-offs. When we read of their amazing sacrifices and achievements, we are sometimes subtly tempted to think that we should emulate them. And when we fail, we feel condemned and guilty.

So we need to take care.

With that caveat, consider George Whitefield (1714–70).

Whitefield was an Anglican evangelist who was used by God in the great Methodist revival of the eighteenth century. He crossed the Atlantic numerous times and was at the forefront of the Great Awakening in the North American colonies. He was a phenomenal preacher, and massive crowds came to hear him. He preached to members of the British aristocracy and American slaves and everyone in between. He often preached three or four times a day. It has been estimated that throughout his life he preached more than 18,000 sermons. That works out as 500 per year for thirty-five years! Remember that this was often in the open air to a congregation of thousands and without the aid of amplification. The constant travel and massive workload stretched his body to its limits.

On 30 September 1770 Whitefield awoke at 2 am with severe breathing problems. He decided to take a few days off to recover, but soon changed his mind. He told his assistant Richard Smith, 'I would rather wear out than rust out.' He prayed for an hour and then fell asleep, only to wake up again at 4 am, barely able to breathe. Later that morning he died fighting for breath.

He was fifty-five years old.

Had his massive workload led to a premature death? Probably. Should he have been wiser with his time and more self-disciplined with his diary? I have to say that I find that question impossible to answer. Here was a man who was utterly consumed by a passion for God and a love for lost people. We are not called to emulate him, but neither should we be overly critical of him. If we are to learn anything, it is that sometimes God calls us to move beyond our comfort zone and serve him sacrificially.

Robert Murray M'Cheyne, whom we met in chapter 6, died at the age of twenty-nine during an epidemic of typhus. Like Whitefield, he worked exceedingly hard, and this may have damaged his health and contributed to his premature death.

M'Cheyne seems to have been aware of this, and towards the end of his life recognized that he might have been more careful. Comparing his body to a horse, he confessed, 'God gave me a gospel to preach and a horse to ride. I've killed the horse, therefore I can no longer preach the gospel.'[8]

Here is a helpful steer. Maximizing our usefulness involves the wise marshalling of our resources. Caring for ourselves is a way of prolonging our usefulness to God.

However, not all good people die young! Read the biography of John Stott, and you will be amazed at his work rate and abiding achievements. This was the result of both exceptional gifts and very hard work. And yet he was able to sustain many years of fruitful ministry because he sensibly marshalled his resources and did not prematurely kill the horse that God had given him to ride. In the afternoons he would regularly take a 'horizontal half-hour' in order to recuperate. Ornithology proved a helpful way of escaping from stressful circumstances for a time. He would mark out special days in his diary with a 'Q', quiet days away from people and alone with God. As a single man, he became a friend, 'Uncle John', to many people. And he continued in faithful service until shortly before his death at the age of ninety.

Caring for ourselves is a way of prolonging our usefulness to God.

And finally we return to the apostle Paul. The words recorded in Acts 20:24 were spoken while he was on his way to Jerusalem. When he arrived, he was arrested and imprisoned for two years. After a hazardous journey to Rome, he spent two more years in prison. Eventually he was released and may have conducted further missionary endeavours. However, he was then re-arrested and imprisoned in Rome. This time there was no release. According to Christian tradition, on the orders of the Emperor Nero, he was led out of the city where he was beheaded in AD 65. He was buried on the Via Ostiensis.

Just before his death, Paul wrote 2 Timothy. Reflecting on over thirty years of ministry and echoing his words in Acts 20, he was able to write,

I have fought the good fight, I have finished the race, I have
kept the faith. Now there is in store for me the crown of
righteousness, which the Lord, the righteous Judge, will award
to me on that day – and not only to me, but also to all who have
longed for his appearing.
(2 Timothy 4:7–8)

We must neither hoard nor waste our lives.

Like Whitefield, it is good to be at full stretch, pushing
ourselves beyond our safety zone. Like M'Cheyne, it is good to
recognize that we must be good stewards of our resources. But
unlike him, we must protect the horse God has given us to ride.
Like John Stott, we should aim at a long life of fruitful ministry.
And like Paul, we need to finish the race that God has set before
us, keeping our eyes on the prize.

Questions

1. Read Acts 20:13–35. What does it tell us about the
   'motivation and method and manner of ministry'?
2. Why do we overwork? Why is exhaustion spiritually
   dangerous?
3. How can self-knowledge help us to avoid making unwise
   mistakes?
4. How do we distinguish a physical problem from a
   spiritual one?
5. With a close and trusted friend, work through the
   questions in the section entitled 'Use sanctified common
   sense'.
6. How do we strike the right balance between sensible
   sacrifice and unwise overcommitment?

13. Be a good steward of pain

The phone rang at 11:30 on a bitterly cold November night.

The moment I picked up the receiver, I knew that I would have to make an emergency visit. During the previous year the man at the other end of the line had had to watch helplessly as one of his children had died of cancer. The child was buried in a lonely grave on a bleak Wiltshire hillside. Your kids shouldn't die before you. It's not fair. It's not right. We had tried to comfort both him and his wife, but it was still early days.

'Can you help me, pastor? I don't know what to do. It's not me – it's my wife. I just don't know what to say to her. Please can you help?'

I promised to be there soon, but I had to clear the ice from the windscreen before driving over to their home. I hadn't been a pastor for long. As I sped through the near-arctic night, I prayed that God would give me the words to say.

When I arrived, the husband ushered me into a brightly lit room where his wife was sitting staring into the fire.

'Thank you for coming over,' she said. 'I'm really sorry I cannot get on top of this. When you have heard what I'm going to say, you'll probably want to throw me out of the church. It's just that I cannot get over the thought of my little boy up on that cold hillside all alone. I know he is in heaven, but I know his body is in that cold hard ground. I want to go to the cemetery and lay a blanket over the grave just to keep him warm. I know it's stupid. I told you that you would want to throw me out of the church, but I can't help it.'

'I don't want to throw you out of the church,' I said. 'I want to hug you and assure you that God loves you more than you can imagine.'

I don't think that she and her husband will ever get over the pain they have experienced. It may fade over the years, but it will never go away.

If you have to have an operation to remove your appendix, you will have a scar for the rest of your life. But most of the time you will be unaware of it. If you lose a leg, you will have to adapt for the rest of your life and always walk with a limp. This will become a daily reality.

The kind of pain felt by this couple is more like the loss of a limb than an appendectomy. They will carry that pain for the rest of their lives, and there will be no easy answers or simplistic comforts.

In this fallen, broken world in which so many people carry a secret wound or an aching scar, God uses suffering to prepare us humbly to serve others. He entrusts us with it so that we can minister to them.

Are you willing to be a good steward of pain?

A qualification of leadership

Leadership does not make us immune to suffering. We suffer like everyone else because we are human beings, living outside the garden. We also suffer because we are followers of a crucified Saviour who told us that suffering would be the price of faithfulness. But on top of that, we suffer because we are leaders. Faithfulness in leadership comes at a price.

You will know by this stage of the book that there is a cost to leading God's people. Some of it stems from external resistance to our message, some from the cost of loving people. If you don't love the people you serve, then you cannot serve them properly. If you do though, you will suffer for it, as their sorrows will become yours too. And if they end up rejecting you, it will feel more painful than the stab of any knife.

Paul writes about the cost of leadership in his letter to the Colossians. He had never visited the church, but while he was in Ephesus, he had sent a man called Epaphras to plant a church in Colossae (Colossians 1:7–8). News had reached him about the baleful influence of heresy, and he wrote to warn them of their danger. False teachers were telling the congregation that they needed more than Christ: Christ is a good start, but he's not enough. If you want to grow as a Christian and come to a 'deeper knowledge' of the faith, you need to push on beyond Jesus.

Paul is furious. This is nonsense. Everything we ever need is in Christ. The fullness of deity resides in the Son of God, and we are complete in him (Colossians 2:9–10). They do not need more than Christ; they need more of Christ.

What gives Paul the right to speak in this way? He has never visited them, admittedly, but they are the indirect result of the ministry in Ephesus, and he has laboured for them in prayer. He has suffered so that this church might come into existence. He refers to this in Colossians 1:24–25:

> Now I rejoice in what I am suffering for you, and I fill up in my flesh what is still lacking in regard to Christ's afflictions, for the sake of his body, which is the church. I have become its servant by the commission God gave me to present to you the word of God in its fullness.

Here Paul links pain and ministry together. Jesus had completed his task through suffering. His sacrifice was unique and unrepeatable. And yet it is a model and pattern we are called to follow if we are to see his church built and his name honoured.

And the sufferings Paul experienced in his body were intense. While in Ephesus he had been pushed to the limit: 'We are hard pressed on every side, but not crushed; perplexed, but not in despair; persecuted, but not abandoned; struck down, but not destroyed' (2 Corinthians 4:8–9).

This suffering is multifaceted: mental, physical, emotional and spiritual.

Are you experiencing this kind of pressure even as you are reading these words today? Is it financial or vocational or relational? Is it the result of old age or illness or accident? Is it caused by stress or overwork or foolish decisions? Or is it the direct results of faithfulness in ministry?

If the answer is 'yes', then God is using this to prepare you for ministry. There is no such thing as pointless pain in the life of the child of God. And there is no such thing as pointless pain in the life of the Christian leader.

I hope this doesn't sound trite or glib, but if we believe in a sovereign God, then we must believe that pain is part of his purpose for our lives. It is not an accident or an aberration or an oversight. It has not reached us by somehow flying under his radar. God sent it and means to use it to fit us for service. We are therefore called to be wise stewards of pain and to allow it to shape and prepare us for ministry.

What is God doing in our pain?

Let me make four suggestions:

1. Suffering deepens our relationship with God

Our relationship with God is more important than what we do for him. Cultivating this relationship is hard work. However much we see it as a priority, we find it a constant battle to keep it at the forefront of our demanding lives. And sometimes it slips.

Pain calls us back to God. Suffering shatters our lives and drives us to our knees. And what do we discover when we get there? We discover the reality of the great truths that we confess. We learn that God really is all that he says he is. We come to see that when God is all you've got, God is all you need.

This is the underlying theme of a score of psalms.

Take Psalm 27, for example. Armies of bloodthirsty men surround David and want to 'devour' him (27:2–3, 6). False witnesses breathe out violence against him (27:11–12). Life is raw and risky. What is David's response? His anguish drives him into the arms of God:

> One thing I ask from the LORD,
>   this only do I seek:
> that I may dwell in the house of the LORD
>   all the days of my life,
> to gaze on the beauty of the LORD
>   and to seek him in his temple.
> (27:4)

David's overwhelming desire is not deliverance or comfort or vindication. None of these things is wrong in itself, and there are moreover plenty of examples of such petitions in the Psalter. However, David rises above his circumstances and recognizes that the greatest need of the hour is an intimate vision of the beauty and glory of the Lord. He wants to seek God's face (27:9–10) and hear God's fatherly instruction (27:11).

The psalm ends with advice for those limping along under the blows of cruel circumstances:

> Wait for the LORD;
>   be strong and take heart
>   and wait for the LORD.
> (27:14)

I remember a particularly tough time in my early years of ministry. I won't go into detail, but I think that it was then I was at my closest to throwing in the towel. I was well and truly knocked off balance. It all seemed so overwhelming and hopeless. I needed some time alone with God, so I escaped to Roundway Down. It is a beautiful hill just outside the little village of Devizes in Wiltshire, the site of a famous battle during the First English Civil War. I had chosen this as a place where I could be alone with God and pour out my heart to him. I had a whole morning alone with my Bible.

That morning prayer didn't come easily. I remember walking along and kicking a couple of tree stumps in order to express my confusion and frustration. Then I turned to Psalm 27 and had an epiphany. Verse 4 stood out – it is still underlined in my battered old Bible. I prayed David's prayer and asked God to show me his beauty. And he did.

I have taught the doctrine of God in many different contexts over the past thirty years. Every time I am overwhelmed by some new insight and driven to worship and adoration. I want to say to Christian leaders, 'Keep your mind active and wrestle with the big subjects. Stay intellectually fresh.' But my knowledge of God is more than the correct grasp of a set of precise theological theses. It is about a relationship. It is experiential and trans-formational. A cool and clinical acquisition of mere facts can mask a dry and barren heart.

Suffering is often the method God uses to wean us from mere intellectual apprehension and drive us into an ever-deepening relationship with himself. When we suffer, Christ becomes our all in all. We discover that everything is a loss compared to knowing Christ (Philippians 3:7–8).

Samuel Rutherford (1600–61) was a Scottish Presbyterian pastor and theologian who acted as one of the Scottish Commissioners to the Westminster Assembly. Suffering for his faithfulness to Christ, including a period of imprisonment, Rutherford wrote of the blessings that knowing Christ had brought to him,

Since He looked upon me, my heart is not my own, He hath
run away to heaven with it.

He enthused,

Jesus Christ came into my prison cell last night, and every
stone flashed like a ruby.

He concluded,

The cross of Christ is the sweetest burden that I ever bore;
it is such a burden as wings are to a bird, or sails to a ship,
to carry me forward to my harbour. Grace grows best in
winter.[1]

Read Rutherford's letters and you will discover the depth of his
devotion and the intensity of his love. Here is a man who knows
his God. And these things grew out of the well-watered soil of
suffering.

I am reminded of a comment I heard from a North Korean
Christian. With many of his friends, he had suffered for his faith
before escaping to the West. Speaking of the effects of persecution on his relationship with God, he said, 'You don't need
to worry about us Koreans. We are like nails. The harder you hit
us, the deeper we go.'

2. Suffering sharpens our understanding of truth

In a similar way, suffering deepens our love and delight in truth.
Not only does it give us a unique and personal insight into the
character of God, but it also sharpens our understanding of
the great truths of the faith that God has revealed in the Bible.
Indeed, suffering focuses the mind wonderfully.

Suddenly we find ourselves living in the pages of Scripture.

Think of Paul's stunning statement in Romans 8:28–30. Here
is a profound affirmation of God's eternal purpose for our lives:

> And we know that in all things God works for the good of those
> who love him, who have been called according to his purpose.
> For those God foreknew he also predestined to be conformed
> to the image of his Son, that he might be the firstborn among
> many brothers and sisters. And those he predestined, he also
> called; those he called, he also justified; those he justified, he
> also glorified.

Behind the sometimes-confusing events of our lives there is a
personal hand at work which is guiding and framing even the
fine details. We have a friend behind the phenomena. Paul is
clear: God is at work in *all* things – not some things or lots of
things or even most things or virtually all things. There is a
purpose in prosperity and adversity, in sickness and in health, in
joys and sorrows, in blessings and trials.

And all things are for our good because the one who plans
them is good and cannot be otherwise (Psalm 100:5). Paul is not
saying that pain is good – how could it be? But the *purpose* is
good. The reasons for which God sends it are always good
reasons. To drive this home, the apostle reminds us of God's
eternal plan. He foreknew us in eternity. This is more than
factual knowledge – it is not that God simply knew about us.
It is relational knowledge, the equivalent of saying that God
loved us before time began. Having set his love on us, he pre-
destined us and called us and justified us. The ultimate outcome
still lies in the future when he will glorify us.

What is at the heart of God's purpose? It is that we should
be transformed into the likeness of Christ, as bearers of the
family likeness (8:29). God sends suffering to bring about this
transformation.

There was once a man who carved beautiful figures in wood.
He could turn his hand to most things, but he specialized in
horses. And the horses he created were stunningly life-like. One
day someone asked him about his technique. How did he
produce such pieces of art? The man thought for a moment and

then confessed, 'I'm not sure really. I just take a block of wood and I look at it for a while. Eventually I see the horse trapped inside. Then I take my knife and I cut away everything that isn't horse.'

God looks at our lives and sees what he wants – a character resembling that of Jesus. He then takes the knife of painful circumstances and the scalpel of adversity and cuts out everything that isn't Christlike. It is in this way that all things work for our good and for God's glory.

It is easy to affirm these truths when the sun is shining and they sound like good theology. It is quite another when our faith and assurance depend upon them. When things seem to fall apart, such truths become more real and vital. And we can teach them with more credibility and insight when people see that our lives depend upon them.

Aeschylus (525–456 BC), one of the great ancient Greek trage-dians whose plays are still performed, grasped something of this:

> He who learns must suffer. And even in our sleep, pain that cannot forget falls drop by drop upon the heart, and in our own despair, against our will, comes wisdom to us by the awful grace of God.[2]

As a pagan, he had no foundation from which he could make sense of such experiences. As Christians, our foundations are secure. Sometimes the 'awful grace of God' leads us to a comprehension of truth which a pain-free existence could never afford.

3. Suffering weans us from sin

Our greatest battle is the battle with sin. How does God break the power of sin in our lives? How does he challenge the arrogance of our hearts and our waywardness?

God purifies our hearts in three ways. Firstly, his Holy Spirit transforms us through the power of the Word of God. Secondly, he puts us in the community of difficult people – 'grace growers' – who force us to exercise patience and love, grace and forgiveness. And then thirdly, he sends adverse circumstances which force us to face up to the waywardness of our hearts.

Pain strips away distractions. It reminds us of our own frailty. It enables us to share in God's holiness (Hebrews 12:10).

Listen to David:

> Before I was afflicted I went astray,
>   but now I obey your word.
> (Psalm 119:67)

Or hear what Paul says:

> We do not want you to be uninformed, brothers and sisters, about the troubles we experienced in the province of Asia. We were under great pressure, far beyond our ability to endure, so that we despaired of life itself. Indeed, we felt we had received the sentence of death. But this happened that we might not rely on ourselves but on God, who raises the dead.
> (2 Corinthians 1:8–9)

And here is Peter:

> Therefore, since Christ suffered in his body, arm yourselves also with the same attitude, because whoever suffers in the body has finished with sin. As a result, they do not live the rest of their earthly lives for evil human desires, but rather for the will of God. For you have spent enough time in the past doing what pagans choose to do – living in debauchery, lust, drunkenness, orgies, carousing and detestable idolatry. They are surprised that you do not join them in their reckless, wild living, and they heap abuse on you.
> (1 Peter 4:1–4)

Pain helps us to identify sin in our hearts. Listen to Brian Hedges:

> Sinful desires can lurk in our hearts unnoticed because those desires are neither threatened nor thwarted. But suffering stirs the calm waters of latent sinful desires. It reveals the true state of our hearts. It's God diagnostic tool, preparing the way of the medicine of gospel truth.[3]

Joni Eareckson Tada became a paraplegic as a result of a diving accident in her teens. She confides in her book *When God Weeps*, 'Before my paralysis, my hands reached for a lot of wrong things and my foot took me into some bad places. After my paralysis, tempting choices were scaled down considerably.'[4]

This is not to say that all suffering is disciplinary – it isn't. But pain does cut us down to size and leave us relying on God.

Suffering undermines our self-reliance. It causes us to have a healthy suspicion of our own gifts and wisdom and resources. It forces us to realize that we need God. If anything of any eternal value is to be accomplished for God, it has to be his work, not ours. He graciously chooses to use us, and suffering hones us so that we are usable.

4. Suffering deepens our sympathy

I was recently invited to hold a series of seminars at a large Christian conference on the subject of living in a broken world. The organizers wanted me to deal with subjects like living with disability, coping with prodigal children and struggling with forgiveness. The first session was on the theme of handling disappointment.

They told me that I should expect about forty participants, but they had printed fifty handouts just to be on the safe side. When I arrived at the venue, I was alone apart from the stewards. With three minutes to go, I had been joined by three elderly ladies and was contemplating a rather-too-intimate discussion on the disappointments of life.

But then people started arriving. There were not forty or fifty – the final number was nearer to 150. We had to put out more seats and rush off more copies of the handouts.

I'd like to say that the size of the crowd was due to the popularity of the speaker. But it wasn't. There were so many people present simply because of the personal relevance of the subject being addressed.

Christian leaders are called to care for hurting people. I think of the story with which I began the chapter. I think of comments made to me over the years:

- 'We had expected to grow old together – why did God take him so soon after retirement?'
- 'All I want to do is work. Why won't anyone give me a job?'
- 'All I ever wanted to be was a mum. I love kids – why can't we have them?'
- 'I was so fit – I never saw this illness coming. It changed everything.'
- 'I was just trying to serve God. Why did he allow life to kick me in the teeth?'

If you are to be an effective and fruitful leader, you will need to minister gently and compassionately into this broken world. And you will soon come to realize that your own sufferings are designed by God to help you to do this.

In 2 Corinthians 1:3–5 Paul expresses it like this:

Praise be to the God and Father of our Lord Jesus Christ, the Father of compassion and the God of all comfort, who comforts us in all our troubles, so that we can comfort those in any trouble with the comfort we ourselves receive from God. For just as we share abundantly in the sufferings of Christ, so also our comfort abounds through Christ.

We suffer and then experience God's comfort so that we can be a blessing and a comfort to others.

David Powlison expresses it like this:

> When you've passed through your own fiery trials, and found
> God to be true to what he says, you have real help to offer.
> You have first-hand experience of both his sustaining grace
> and his purposeful design. He has kept you through pain; he has
> reshaped you more into his image . . . what you are experiencing
> from God, you can give away in increasing measure to others.
> You are learning both the tenderness and the clarity necessary
> to help sanctify another person's deepest distress.[5]

My own story

My own ministry is divided into two clear and distinct stages.

I became a pastor in 1982, and for the first ten years my wife and I served in the church mentioned in the introduction to this book. Edrie was fit and healthy and vivacious. She was the most life-affirming person I had ever met, a brilliant support to my ministry and a marvellous mum to our (then) three children. Life was good, and we often commented on how bountiful God had been to us.

Then everything changed.

In 1991 Edrie became pregnant again. It was a difficult pregnancy, but she seemed to come through the worst of it. But as 1992 dawned – the anniversary of our ten years in Christian leadership – Edrie became seriously ill. She experienced debilitating weakness and a loss of balance and coordination. She was so unwell that the doctors feared the worst.

Eventually she gave birth to our fourth child, and they zapped her with steroids and hoped that she might recover. She never has done. She now lives with a degenerative illness. There has never been a diagnosis, so we are left with describing it as an unidentified neurological condition similar to multiple sclerosis. There have been periods of excruciating pain and times of near despair.

And yet this has been the single greatest influence on my ministry, shaping my leadership more than any other single thing. Walking with my wife through this dark valley has had a profound influence on every aspect of our lives, including our service for God.[6]

Invest your suffering

People are not always sensitive:

'It's been such a long time – you must have got used to it by now!'

Used to coming home to find my beautiful wife has had yet another fall and is wreathed in bruises? Used to having to soothe away the agony of an excruciating pain attack? Used to trying to comfort her when life seems impossibly sad?

Of course not! I hate it. I'm not some weird kind of masochist who cannot wait for the next round of pain.

But if you ask me whether God has used this to bless us and equip us to serve others, the answer is a resounding 'yes'. From a very early stage we learned that pain could have a positive influence on ministry. If we correctly 'invest our suffering', God will bring spiritual fruit out of what seems to be the most barren and unpromising ground.

Part two of my ministry – over twenty years now – has been deeply influenced by our domestic circumstances. It has limited some of my movements and terminated opportunities. At the same time, it has transformed my preaching, deepened my pastoral insights and thrown me into complete dependence on God.

The challenge of this book is the challenge to remain fresh and sharp in our leadership. Suffering can work in one of two ways:

it can wear us down and cause us to lose our edge, or it can sharpen us and deepen our dependence on God. The challenge we face is to refuse to allow it to make us bitter, but to see it as a useful tool in God's hands to shape us for leadership.

Are you willing to be a good steward of pain?

Questions

1. What lessons has God taught you through pain? How have they helped you in your leadership?
2. 'There is a cost to leading God's people. Some of it stems from external resistance to our message, some from the cost of loving people. If you don't love the people you serve, then you cannot serve them properly. If you do, though, you will suffer for it, as their sorrows will become your sorrows too. And if they end up rejecting you, it will feel more painful than the stab of any knife.' Is this true? What are the other costs of leadership? What are the blessings that compensate for this?
3. 'There is no future in frustration.'[7] How do we avoid becoming frustrated or bitter leaders?
4. Study Paul's experience of ministry in 1 Corinthians 2:1–5. How did he feel when he arrived at Corinth? Where did he place his confidence?
5. Reread the early section of this chapter. What comfort might you have given to the grieving couple described there?

14. Keep an eye on the prize

Eric Liddell was born to missionary parents on 16 January 1902 in Tientsin, northern China. He went on to play rugby for Scotland and to represent Britain at the 1924 Paris Olympics. His story is retold in the 1981 film *Chariots of Fire*.

Because of his strong Christian convictions about Sunday observance, Eric was forced to withdraw from the 100 metres, because one of the heats was on a Sunday. He competed in the 400 metres instead – a big ask for an athlete who specialized in shorter distances. At the starting block a masseur from the American Olympic Team slipped a piece of paper into his hand with a quotation from the Bible: 'Those who honour me I will honour' (1 Samuel 2:30). Although he was not experienced in the longer distance, Liddell won the gold medal and set a new world record time of 47.6 seconds.

From 1925 to 1943 Liddell served as a missionary in northern China. When the Japanese invaded China, Liddell faced many dangers. In 1943 he was interned at the Weihsien Internment Camp along with other missionaries from the China Inland Mission.

Suffering from exhaustion, malnutrition and a brain tumour, Liddell died on 21 February 1945, five months before liberation.

Referring to his love for Christ, Liddell's last words were: 'It's complete surrender.' It was later revealed that he had refused an opportunity to leave the camp, giving up his place for a pregnant woman.

When asked about the strategy at the 1924 Olympics that had won him the race, Liddell was reported to have answered, 'I ran the first 200 metres as hard as I possibly could. Then, for the second 200 metres, with God's help, I ran harder.'

Running the race

Liddell's words are a great metaphor for Christian leadership. It is neither a sprint nor a middle-distance race. In fact, it is even more than a gruelling marathon. It is a lifelong commitment to following Jesus Christ, wherever he leads.

Sometimes leadership feels like an exhausting slog. How does the runner keep going through all the gruelling hours of training and the constant call to sacrifice? It is the prospect of winning the prize and lifting the trophy. As he runs around the training track on a cold, wet, miserable Wednesday morning in November when most sensible people are still in bed, he imagines standing on the podium as the strains of the national anthem sound out and the precious gold medal is placed around his neck.

And it is the same in Christian ministry. We are running in order to win a prize.

We may feel a little uncomfortable about this. Surely I serve God because I love him and want to please him? It is love and gratitude that drive me. Yes, but there are other legitimate motives to keep us going too. The Bible is quite unembarrassed about setting the prize before us. In his well-known parable of the talents Jesus promises rewards for those who invest their gifts in the kingdom and look for gospel growth. He is scathing about those who play it safe and do not engage in gospel enterprise (Matthew 25:14–29).

Paul picks up the warning when he writes to the Corinthians. They must be careful about how they serve God and in particular about the materials they use:

> If anyone builds on this foundation using gold, silver, costly stones, wood, hay or straw, their work will be shown for what it is, because the Day will bring it to light. It will be revealed with fire, and the fire will test the quality of each person's work. If what has been built survives, the builder will receive a reward. If it is burned up, the builder will suffer loss but yet will be saved – even though only as one escaping through the flames. (1 Corinthians 3:12–15)

There is no greater calamity than a wasted life.

Winning the prize

Peter urges church leaders to care for the flock, 'not because you must, but because you are willing, as God wants you to be; not pursuing dishonest gain, but eager to serve; not lording it over those entrusted to you, but being examples to the flock' (1 Peter 5:2–3).

What is their motive? He points them forward to the return of Christ: '. . . when the Chief Shepherd appears, you will receive the crown of glory that will never fade away' (5:4).

There is no greater calamity than a wasted life.

We are not to work for earthly fame or glory, nor for material gain and comfort, but for the prize that Jesus will give. Sometimes ministry is demanding, and we feel overwhelmed by the pressure. Sometimes it is tedious and banal, and we feel smothered. What are we to do in such circumstances? We are to lift up our eyes and fix them on Jesus and the rewards he will bestow.

This is what enabled Paul to stay true in the crucible of suffering which was his ministry:

> For I am already being poured out like a drink offering, and the time for my departure is near. I have fought the good fight, I have finished the race, I have kept the faith. Now there is in store for me the crown of righteousness, which the Lord, the righteous Judge, will award to me on that day – and not only to me, but also to all who have longed for his appearing.
> (2 Timothy 4:6–8)

But what exactly is the prize?

'This world is not our home'

One of the great tragedies of the twenty-first-century church is that we have forgotten that we are only pilgrims here. The world is the bridge we pass over in order to reach the joy and blessings of our eternal home. I live in England. Two of my gorgeous little granddaughters live in South Wales. To reach them, we have to cross the Severn Bridge. It is a mightily impressive bridge, but I never stop my car halfway across in order to admire it. It is not my destination. I'm longing for the embrace of my grand-daughters. I'm only crossing the bridge to get to my ultimate destination.

'This world is not my home; I'm just passing through.'[1] The Bible has a very world-affirming theology, and assures us that one day there will be a new heavens and a new earth. In the end, this world will be renewed and restored. However, having said this, we need to remember that this world in its current fallen condition is not our final destination.

We are to enjoy the legitimate pleasures of the world and to do all that we can to make it a better place, but in the end nothing in this world can hold ultimate value for us. Nothing here can finally and fully satisfy us. Nothing is perfect. Every marriage, every relationship, every ministry, every church is flawed. These gracious gifts from a generous God may bring joy and pleasure for a while, but they are not of ultimate worth. If we are not careful, we can receive the gifts and forget the Giver. Temporary joys must be tempered by the contemplation of ultimate delights.

When the disciples returned to tell Jesus of the successes of their missionary trip, they focused on the amazing fact that even the evil spirits were submissive to them. Jesus is glad to hear this, but he warns them, 'However, do not rejoice that the spirits submit to you, but rejoice that your names are written in heaven' (Luke 10:20).

We may know some successes in ministry faithfully undertaken in the name of Jesus, but even these can cause us to forget the final and full goal of our lives.

We need to keep our eyes on the prize.

But can we be more specific? What exactly is the nature of the prize we strive for?

'The bride eyes not her garment'

The New Testament is rather guarded about the way in which it describes the new heaven and the new earth. Revelation 21:1 – 22:6 speaks of a real place where resurrected people enjoy eternal bliss. However, the passage is full of symbols that point beyond themselves to realities which are too sublime for our minds to grasp quite yet.

Nonetheless, we can still be clear in our hope. We will have new bodies in which there is no tendency to decay and no residue of sin. We will experience the delightful reunion with those we have loved and lost for a while. We can anticipate a new heavens and a new earth in which every scar of sin and every stain of evil is removed. We will enter into the fullness of all our created potential – to reign as vice-regents in God's world as we were always intended to do.

But most of all, we will see Jesus. Our greatest hope is to know him fully, and our most powerful longing to be with him forever in an unclouded fellowship which transcends time itself. In the words of a great hymn based on the writings of Samuel Rutherford,

> The bride eyes not her garment,
> But her dear bridegroom's face;
> I will not gaze at glory,
> But on my King of grace;
> Not at the crown He giveth,
> But on His piercèd hand:
> The Lamb is all the glory
> In Emmanuel's land.[2]

What is at the heart of the Christian hope? In the end, it is the hope of seeing Jesus.

'For to me, to live . . .'

Paul knows this as he sits in a cell in Rome waiting to go on trial before Nero. He writes as a seasoned leader to a group of Christians in Philippi whom he holds close to his heart, 'For to me, to live is Christ and to die is gain' (Philippians 1:21).

Christ dominates his horizon. In spite of adverse circumstances, this letter is a wonderful manifesto of Christian joy. What gives him such confidence and joy in the midst of trials? What is the secret of sacrificial ministry? The answer is simple.

My leadership is for Jesus. I love him and live for him and long to please him. I praise him as my Saviour and adore him as my God. I follow him as my Master and trust him as my older Brother. I preach him and serve him and am utterly satisfied with him. So when people strip me of present comforts and earthly hopes, I find my joy in him.

And if this is true, it follows that 'to die is gain'. To depart from this life is, for the apostle, to enter into the presence of Christ. It is to see him with no veil between.

How does this affect his present thinking as he faces the uncertainties of a Roman trial?

> If I am to go on living in the body, this will mean fruitful
> labour for me. Yet what shall I choose? I do not know! I am
> torn between the two: I desire to depart and be with Christ,
> which is better by far; but it is more necessary for you that
> I remain in the body.
> (1:22–24)

If you push me, says Paul, I am not afraid to die. In fact, I am looking forward to it. At my death I will not be lost. I will depart and be with Christ. What could be better? The only thing that holds me back is my love for you. I want to serve you, and it is necessary for you that I stay in the body.

The word 'depart' was used to describe the demobbing of a Roman legionnaire. Imagine a Roman soldier stationed on the edge of the Empire, perhaps on the wild northern frontier of Britannia. It is cold and wet and barren and dangerous. He dreams of home – his little farm in Calabria where his plump wife and noisy children are waiting for him. At home the sun always shines, and the grapes are succulent, and rebellious tribesmen are miles away beyond the borders of the Empire. One day the news arrives. His time of service is completed. The Empire is grateful for his sacrifice and is about to put a small fortune in his pocket and send him home.

How does he feel? Overjoyed! Ecstatic! He cannot wait!

This is how Paul felt about his departure. It is to be away from the body, but it is to be at home with the Lord. Here is a consummation devoutly to be wished.

The prize worth securing

Paul picks this up in Philippians 3 where he again returns to his favourite metaphor of the runner:

> Not that I have already obtained all this, or have already arrived at my goal, but I press on to take hold of that for which Christ Jesus took hold of me. Brothers and sisters, I do not consider myself yet to have taken hold of it. But one thing I do: forgetting what is behind and straining towards what is ahead, I press on towards the goal to win the prize for which God has called me heavenwards in Christ Jesus.
> (3:12–14)

He is still only part-way round the circuit. There is a long way to go. The goal is in sight, but he isn't there yet. So what does he do? He forgets past blessings or achievements or failures – we all have our fair share of those – and he presses on. Like Eric Liddell, he has run the first part of the race as fast as his legs can take him. But that's not enough. Now, with God's help, he will run the last part even more quickly.

And he will keep his eye on the prize (3:14). The word for 'prize' refers to the laurel crown placed on the head of victorious athletes. It was sometimes placed on a pole next to the finishing line so that the runner could see it as he rounded the last bend. The sight of it spurred him on.

And this is what spurs Paul on. He can see the prize before him, and it gives him a fresh determination and new zeal to press on. He describes the prize as calling him heavenwards. At the end of the chapter he spells it out:

> But our citizenship is in heaven. And we eagerly await a Saviour from there, the Lord Jesus Christ, who, by the power that enables him to bring everything under his control, will transform our lowly bodies so that they will be like his glorious body.
> (3:20–21)

We are looking for Jesus. He is the only prize worth securing. He is the treasure which is so valuable that we should be willing to sacrifice anything to gain him. His words, 'Well done, good and faithful servant' (Matthew 25:21, 23), are the only ones worth hearing. What keeps us going in the cut and thrust of Christian leadership? It is the prospect of being with Christ forever in that place where faith gives way to sight, and hope receives its final reward, and love remains forever satisfied with the object of its devotion.

The riddle of the sands

Let's return to the question we started with: how do we maintain our first love and not lose our freshness? How does service remain joyful?

Through the prophet Jeremiah, God pinpoints two sins that his people, in their catastrophic stupidity, have committed:

> My people have committed two sins:
> They have forsaken me,
>   the spring of living water,
> and have dug their own cisterns,
>   broken cisterns that cannot hold water.
> (Jeremiah 2:13)

Here is the riddle of the sands.

Imagine a man slowly traversing a blisteringly hot desert. The sun beats mercilessly on his head, and he has nothing to drink to relieve his distress. His tongue is swollen. His lips are cracked. Every pore in his body cries out for moisture.

Finally, he reaches the other side of the desert. Before him is a clear choice. To the left is a dry and broken cistern. At its base there is a residue of scum-covered water. It is filthy and meagre. If he throws himself face down into the mud, he can suck a little moisture through his teeth, but the prospect is frankly revolting.

To his right there is a beautiful icy-cold fountain of sparkling water. A spray of mist envelops it. The noise of the water gushing from the fountain and cascading onto the surrounding rocks is the most sublime symphony he has ever heard.

Here is the riddle: will he turn to the broken cistern or to the sparkling fountain? It's not really a riddle at all, is it? It is a 'no-brainer'. Without thinking, his instinct will drive him to the spring of water. We would doubt the sanity of anyone who chose otherwise.

And yet . . .

Pardon our stupidity

This is what Israel had done. And this is the insanity of sin. They preferred the empty cisterns of useless idols to the magnificent delight of knowing and loving and serving God. And before we are too quick to condemn them, we too need to be aware of this same tendency in our own hearts. We turn our leadership or our preaching or our youth ministry or our musical talent into an idol. Then we wonder why our love for Christ has grown cold and the ministry has become a soul-sapping duty. We are trying to satisfy our thirst in the wrong place.

How do we combat this tendency? We need to remember the ultimate goal to which all our desires and yearnings must aspire. Our hope is the hope of heaven. Our goal is the delight of heaven. Our ambition is to drink of the heavenly fountain which will satisfy us forever. And the centre of all these hopes and dreams and expectations is God himself. Our goal is God.

When leadership is painful and we feel crushed by the cost of service, only this hope can lighten our burdens and cheer our hearts. When we feel tempted to love the service of God more than the God whom we serve, only this hope will challenge our stupidity and rebuke our wandering. When we have preached our last sermon or led our last youth group or chaired our last leaders' meeting or taught our final Sunday school lesson, this hope will be just as powerful and real and sustaining as it has ever been.

John Stephen Akhwari

John Stephen Akhwari is not as well known as Eric Liddell, but perhaps he should be.

He was born in 1938 in Mbulu, Tanganyika. He represented his country in the 1968 Olympics in Mexico City, running in the marathon. The high altitude caused him to suffer a severe attack of cramp. At the 19-km point, with another 23 km to go, he fell to the pavement, dislocating his knee and damaging his shoulder. The medics wanted him to retire, but he refused. He limped on for over 2 hours, finishing the race in 3 hours, 25 minutes and 27 seconds, long after the last competitor. Only a few spectators were left in the stadium, but they gave him a standing ovation as he hobbled round the track for the last lap.

When he was asked why he continued running, he said, 'My country did not send me 5,000 miles to start the race; they sent me 5,000 miles to finish the race.'

Like the words of Eric Liddell, these form an excellent metaphor for Christian ministry.

Jesus Christ, the eternal Son of God and the darling of heaven, left the glory of the Father's side to be incarnate, to live a perfect life and suffer the agonies of the cross in order to redeem us. We belong to him. In his infinite mercy, he has not only rescued us, but recruited us into his service. We have been sent into the world to serve him.

And remember, he didn't send you to start a race – he sent you to finish it.

Questions

1. What place does the expectation of rewards play in the leader's life?
2. Someone has said that compared with love and faith, hope is a kind of poor relation. Why do we neglect hope? Why is it vital to our spiritual health?
3. Read 1 Peter 1:3–5. What is the foundation and content of our hope?
4. How can the contemplation of our hope prepare us for the demands of leadership now? How can it keep us fresh and vibrant in our experience?
5. What has God given you to complete? Make a list and pray through it.

Keep going!

Further reading

Leadership and its challenges

Julian Hardyman, *Idols: God's Battle for our Hearts* (IVP, 2010).
R. Kent and Barbara Hughes, *Liberating Ministry from the Success Syndrome* (Crossway, 1987).
Dave Kraft, *Mistakes Leaders Make* (Crossway, 2012).
Albert Mohler, *The Conviction to Lead: 25 Principles for Leadership that Matters* (Baker, 2012).
Paul David Tripp, *Dangerous Calling: The Unique Challenges of Pastoral Ministry* (IVP, 2012).

Integrity

Jonathan Lamb, *Integrity: Leading with God Watching* (IVP, 2006).

Servant leadership

Phil Ryken, *Loving the Way Jesus Loves* (Crossway / IVP UK, 2012).
John Stott, *Calling Christian Leaders: Biblical Models of Church, Gospel and Ministry* (IVP, 2002).
Chua Wee Hian, *Learning to Lead: Biblical Leadership Then and Now* (IVP, 1987).

Holy living

Christopher Ash, *Pure Joy: Rediscover Your Conscience* (IVP,
2012).
Tim Chester, *You Can Change: God's Transforming Power for
Our Sinful Behaviour and Negative Emotions* (IVP, 2008).
Kevin DeYoung, *The Hole in Our Holiness* (Crossway, 2012).
J. C. Ryle, *Holiness: Its Nature, Hindrances, Difficulties and Roots*
(Alban Publishing, 2007).

Training other leaders

Marcus Honeysett, *Fruitful Leaders: How to Make, Grow, Love
and Keep Them* (IVP, 2011).

Busyness and priorities

Tim Chester, *The Busy Christian's Guide to Busyness* (IVP, 2008).
Kevin DeYoung, *Crazy Busy* (IVP, 2013).

Coping with pain

Don Carson, *How Long, O Lord? Reflections on Suffering and Evil*
(IVP, 1991).
Paul Mallard, *Invest Your Suffering: Unexpected Intimacy with a
Loving God* (IVP, 2013).

Marriage

Christopher Ash, *Married for God: Making Your Marriage the Best
It Can Be* (IVP, 2007).

John Piper, *This Momentary Marriage: A Parable of Permanence* (IVP, 2009).

Family

Ann Benton, *Teenagers: Biblical Wisdom for Parents* (IVP, 2009).
Ann Benton and friends, *The Minister's Wife: Privileges, Pressures and Pitfalls* (IVP, 2012).
Amanda Robbie, *The Ministry of a Messy House: Grace in Place of Guilt* (IVP, 2013).

Perseverance

Peter Brain, *Going the Distance: How to Stay Fit for a Lifetime of Ministry* (Matthias Media, 2004).
J. I. Packer, *Finishing Our Course with Joy: Ageing with Hope* (IVP, 2014).

Notes

Introduction

1. Taken from the hymn, 'God Moves in a Mysterious Way', by William Cowper, written in 1774. Cowper suffered from chronic depression, and the hymn reflects his confidence in God in the midst of adverse circumstances.

1. When love turns cold

1. This is reported by the Church Father Jerome in his commentary on Galatians 6:10. John was carried into the congregation in the arms of his disciples and was unable to say anything except, 'Little children, love one another.' At last, wearied that he always spoke the same words, they asked, 'Master, why do you always say this?'

   'Because,' he replied, 'it is the Lord's command, and if this only is done, it is enough.' See John R. W. Stott, *The Epistles of John*, Tyndale New Testament Commentaries (Eerdmans, 1964), p. 49, citing St Jerome's commentary on Galatians 6.

2. From the hymn by Samuel J. Stone (1839–1900), 'The Church's One Foundation' (1866).

3. From the hymn by Augustus M. Toplady (1740–78), 'Rock of Ages, Cleft for Me' (1763).

2. Know that we are loved

1. John Owen, *Communion with God* (Banner of Truth, 1991), p. 16. Owen continues: 'Many saints have no greater burden in their

lives than that their hearts do not constantly delight and rejoice in God. There is still in them a resistance to walking close with God . . . So do this: set your thoughts on the eternal love of the Father and see if your heart is not aroused to delight in him. Sit down for a while at this delightful spring of living water and you will soon find its streams sweet and delightful. You who used to run from God will not now be able, even for a second, to keep at any distance from him' (pp. 17–18).

2. Hymn by William Rees (1802–83), 'Here Is Love Vast as the Ocean'.

3. These words are from 'The Power of the Cross' by Stuart Townend and Keith Getty. Copyright © 2005 Thankyou Music.

3. Rejoice in the Lord

1. I have written more about this in *Invest Your Suffering: Unexpected Intimacy with a Loving God* (IVP, 2013).

2. George Müller, *A Narrative of Some of the Lord's Dealings with George Müller – Written by Himself*, 2 vols (Dust and Ashes, 2003), vol. 2, pp. 730–731.

3. Ibid.

4. From a hymn by C. H. Spurgeon, 'Amidst Us Our Belovèd Stands' (1866).

4. Count the cost

1. Chua Wee Hian, *Learning to Lead: Biblical Leadership Then and Now* (IVP, 1987), p. 35.

5. Fear God, not people

1. This quote is from Dorothy Bernard (1890–1955). She was an American actress of the silent era who appeared in eighty-seven films between 1908 and 1956. It has also been attributed to Karl Barth, the famous Swiss theologian.

2. John Piper, *The Supremacy of God in Preaching* (Kingsway, 1990), p. 9.

6. Take time to be holy

1. Alec Motyer, *The Message of Exodus: The Days of Our Pilgrimage*, in the Bible Speaks Today series (IVP, 2005), p. 200.
2. J. C. Ryle, *Holiness: Its Nature, Hindrances, Difficulties and Roots* (Evangelical Press, 1979), p. 39.
3. Andrew Bonar, *Memoir and Remains of Robert Murray M'Cheyne* (Banner of Truth, 1987).
4. Quoted by Charles Spurgeon in *Lectures to My Students* (Banner of Truth, 2008), p. 94.

7. Take more time to be holy

1. This quote has a number of possible derivations. What we can say with certainty is that it comes from the Fundamentalist tradition of the United States of America. Fundamentalists put a strong emphasis on what they considered to be clear external evidences of holiness. Teetotalism, abstention from any use of tobacco and shunning people who might not share your strong convictions used to be vital signs of a holy life.
2. The Bible Speaks Today volumes are a series of expositions, based on the books of the Old and New Testaments, and on Bible themes that run through the whole of Scripture. They are published by Inter-Varsity Press, Nottingham.

8. Guard your marriage

1. http://en.wikipedia.org/wiki/juggling.
2. This piece of advice from Scripture can be found in Ephesians 4:26.

9. Build godly relationships

1. John Oswald Sanders, *Spiritual Leadership: A Commitment to Excellence for Every Believer* (STL, 1967), p. 107.
2. Ibid., p. 108.
3. John Blanchard, *More Gathered Gold* (Evangelical Press, 1986), p. 43.
4. *Band of Brothers*, HBO (2001), based on Stephen E. Ambrose's book of the same title (1992).

5. Posted on CNN website, 7 September 2001: http://edition.cnn. com/2001/SHOWBIZ/TV/09/07/band.brothers/.
6. Maxie Dunnam, Gordon MacDonald and Donald W. McCullough, *Mastering Personal Growth* (Multnomah, 1992).

10. Preach the gospel to your own heart

1. *The Works of John Bunyan* (Halcyon Press, 2009). See also Chris Tiegreen, *The One Year Walk with God Devotional: Wisdom from the Bible to Renew Your Mind* – 24 September (Tyndale House Publishers, 2012).
2. C. S. Lewis, *The Problem of Pain* (William Collins, 2012).
3. As the good Shepherd, Jesus calls his sheep into the safety and security of the fold.
4. Charles Wesley, 'Jesus, Lover of My Soul' (1740).
5. You can read more about 'Rabbi' Duncan in A. Moody Stuart, *The Life of John Duncan* (Banner of Truth, 1991).

11. Control your diary

1. See John Wesley, *The Journal of John Wesley*, ed. Robert Backhouse (Hodder & Stoughton, 1993).
2. J. Ortberg, 'The Last Taboo: Today's Unforgivable Sin that No Leader Dare Confess', *Leadership Magazine*, spring 1994, pp. 80–85.

12. Remember you are human

1. You can read more about this in Paul Mallard, *Invest Your Suffering* (IVP, 2013).
2. C. S. Lewis, *The Four Loves* (Harcourt Brace Jovanovich, 1960), pp. 169–170.
3. Quoted in Paul D. Robbins (ed.), *When It's Time to Move: A Guide to Changing Churches*, The Leadership Library (Waco Books, 1985), p. 154.
4. Ibid.
5. You can read more about the ministry of Martyn Lloyd-Jones in Iain Murray, *The Life of Martyn Lloyd-Jones – 1899–1981* (Banner of Truth, 2013).

6. Robert Grant, 'Oh, Worship the King, All Glorious Above', based on a reworking of lyrics by William Kethe in the Genevan Psalter of 1561.

7. Dr Archibald D. Hart, 'The Minister's Life: Coping with the Emotional Hazards of Ministry' (Fuller Theological Seminary notes).

8. E. Skoglund, *Burning Out for God* (IVP, 1988), p. 12.

13. Be a good steward of pain

1. You can read Rutherford's story in Faith Cook, *Grace in Winter* (Banner of Truth, 1989).

2. This quote is from *Agamemnon* 1.177. Bobby Kennedy used this quote in his speech on the dreadful night in 1968 when he had to inform a gathered crowd of the assassination of Martin Luther King.

3. See Brian G. Hedges, *Christ Formed in You: The Power of the Gospel for Personal Change* (Shepherd Press, 2010), pp. 222–234.

4. Joni Eareckson Tada, *When God Weeps* (Zondervan, 2000), p. 45.

5. David Powlison, in John Piper and Justin Taylor (eds.), *Suffering and the Sovereignty of God* (Crossway, 2007), p. 166.

6. I have written on this subject at greater length in *Invest Your Suffering* (IVP, 2013). The title describes what Edrie and I have tried to do over the last few years.

7. Don Carson, *How Long, O Lord?* (IVP, 1991), p. 73.

14. Keep an eye on the prize

1. The title of an old Negro spiritual song.

2. Anne R. Cousin, 'The Sands of Time Are Sinking', *The Christian Treasury*, 1857. Published by the authority of the General Assembly of the Presbyterian Church in the USA, 1895.

also by Paul Mallard

Invest Your Suffering

Unexpected intimacy with a loving God
Paul Mallard

ISBN: 978-1-78359-006-3
192 pages, paperback

'Let me be honest, during the last twenty years there have been times when my faith has seemed frail and fragile and almost ready to collapse. I have struggled with seeing my wife stripped of her dignity and reduced by her agony. I have doubted all kinds of things. I have exploded and lashed out. I do not like what is happening to my sweetheart one little bit. Chronic illness never goes away. Come on, realistically, how much more can we take?' says Paul Mallard. 'But one thing I have never doubted is that, in the darkest circumstances, we were only ever in the hands of God. That has been the ultimate source of comfort and hope.'

As Paul Mallard knows only too well, the crucible of suffering is a horrible place to be. But lessons learned there can be powerful and memorable. And it was there that Paul and Edrie experienced unexpected intimacy with a loving God who is no stranger to suffering. They feel personally challenged to use their experience and insights to help fellow sufferers too.

'Absolutely riveting! ... The best explanation of the suffering, death and resurrection of Christ that I have ever read.' Fiona Castle

Available from your local Christian bookshop or **www.thinkivp.com**

Dangerous Calling

*The unique challenges
of pastoral ministry*
Paul David Tripp

ISBN: 978-1-84474-602-6
224 pages, large paperback

Paul David Tripp is concerned about the state of pastoral culture. He is not only concerned about the spiritual life of the pastor, but with the very people who train him, call him, relate to him and, if necessary, restore him.

Dangerous Calling reveals the truth that the culture surrounding our pastors is spiritually unhealthy – an environment that actively undermines the well-being and efficacy of our church leaders and thus the entire church body. This book offers both diagnosis and cure for issues that impact on every member and church leader, and gives solid strategies for fighting the war that rages not only in the momentous moments of ministry, but also in the mundane day-by-day life of every pastor.

'Few would regard a pastor's role as a dangerous calling, but few people are as qualified and insightful as Paul Tripp to penetrate the snares and potential pitfalls associated with pastoral ministry ... This excellent volume should be read, reread and applied.' Terry Virgo